On Top of the World

29 April 2004

On Top
of the
World

REBECCA STEPHENS

To Helen,

On the opening of the 6th

Form centre.

Very best wishes

Rebecca Stephens

First published 1994 by Macmillan London

Reprinted 2003 by Rebecca Stephens

ISBN 0 9544476 0 3

1 3 5 7 9 8 6 4 2

A CIP catalogue record for this book is available from
the British Library

Typeset by CentraServe Limited, Cambridge
Printed by Creative Print and Design Group, Harmondsworth, Middlesex

For John, without whom my climbing
Everest would have remained a dream

Acknowledgements

———•◦•———

My thanks to all those who supported the DHL British 40th Anniversary Everest Expedition 1993 and especially our principal sponsor, *DHL International UK Ltd.*

William Essex, my editor on Resident Abroad, for putting up with years of my burbling. Georgina Morley and Hazel Orme at Pan Macmillan for their patience. Neville Shulman for steering a path through right and wrong. Peter Earl for being a pathological optimist and for coming up with the crazy idea in the first place. And my mother for supporting me to the last.

A full list of sponsors is included at the end of the text.

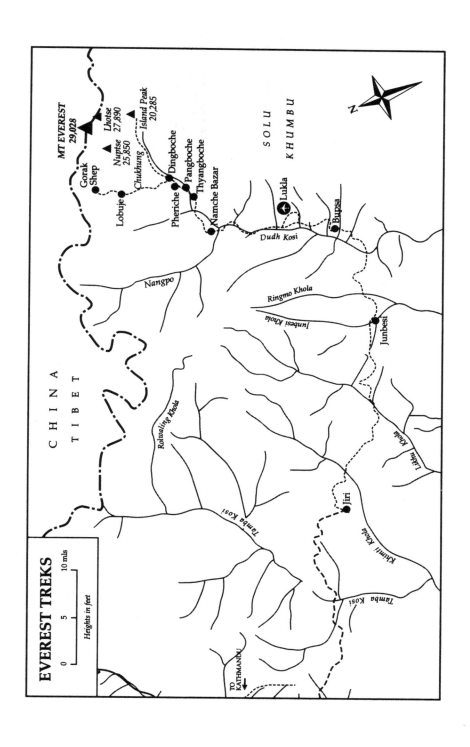

Chapter One

THE SOUTH COL is a strange and lonely place. It lies high, high up on Everest's southern flank, a secret plateau, barren and hostile, swept clean of snow by the ceaseless westerly winds. It is a place inimical to mankind. The air is thin, and the oxygen so deficient that if anyone is foolish enough to go there, they must do so carrying their own supply of oxygen in canisters upon their back, like a deep-sea diver. Should their oxygen supply run dry, they will die, not instantly, but in three days, maybe four – for no other reason than it is too high. There are no rescue services on the South Col; at 26,000 feet, it is too high for a helicopter to fly. The only other people who might be there are other climbers, for this is the launch pad for the pinnacle of Mount Everest. From the South Col, it is possible to climb to the summit and down again in a night and a day. It is the highest and final camp on the southern side of Everest.

I was there, huddled in a small domed tent with John Barry, the leader of our expedition, when I heard a cry: 'British people! British people!' It was dark, about ten o'clock in the evening of 10 May 1993. Our intention had been to pack our rucksacks in an hour or so, and with two Sherpas,

Ang Passang and Kami Tchering, camped in a neighbouring tent, endeavour to climb to the summit. The night before, at eleven o'clock, we had watched a companion, Harry Taylor, leave the Col for a summit bid, alone, and without the aid of bottled oxygen. We feared for his life. He had been gone twenty-three hours – far longer than was considered ample time to climb to the top and safely down again – and still he had not returned. Until now.

'Pull him in!' cried John.

At the door of our tent were two well-meaning Basques, chattering madly, and, at their feet, Harry, slumped on the ground like a sack of old potatoes. I grabbed a handful of battered, down suit and with a strength born of anxiety, heaved him, prostrate, into the tent. Thank God he was alive! He lay on his back, his head and shoulders resting where they had landed, on my lap. He was exhausted, shivering with cold. I held him, fluffed up a sleeping bag around him and held him some more, willing warmth into his bones. 'A drink, please,' he muttered.

John was hurrying a brew. With the billy in one hand, he rootled among the odd gloves, the curled-up socks, the down jackets, head torches, the dead teabags, empty soup packets and spilt sugar that lay strewn, disgustingly, around the tent, for a spare oxygen mask with the other, and handed it to me. 'Now take that,' I said, planting it on Harry's face, 'and breathe deep.'

But it was liquid that his body was desperate for, so I gave him a drink, and eventually we established a rhythm: a few sips of unappetizing tepid water, then oxygen; more water, and oxygen, until the shivering subsided, and the pace no longer was a panic.

It was strange to see Harry like this. He's a tough man, a soldier, SAS and all that, and on the mountain he has a reputation of being one who strides strong and fast, particularly at high altitude. I had watched him over the past few weeks, powering out of sight like an express train hurrying to catch up on lost time. He's an Everest veteran; he had climbed on the mountain five times, on hard routes and in the winter, and always high. And now this. 'So tell us, Harry, what happened?'

He was perfectly coherent. He said he had developed snow-blindness. He had fallen, lost a crampon and fallen again, 100 feet or so, and been found by the two Basques floundering hopelessly in the snow. 'I've banged myself about a bit, hips and everything,' he said.

I gave him another drink. 'And did you make it?' I asked. It seemed a silly question, somehow.

'Yeah,' he said, 'I made it.'

I T WAS always assumed, I think, that Harry would make it to the top. Of all of us on the team, it was he, with five Everest expeditions behind him (all on far harder routes), with his extraordinary, almost freakish ability to acclimatize to extreme altitude, with his single-mindedness, his self-contained assurance, who was considered, above us all, to have the best chance of success. 'Three weeks,' he pronounced, on arrival at Base Camp, 'and we'll bag this and be off.' I don't think it struck me then quite what an exceptional achievement it was. Harry had climbed Everest without bottled oxygen. He was only the second Briton to do so, Stephen Venables having been the first, in 1988. Both, in

Harry's words, were 'fine-lining' – walking on the knife-edge between life and death. Venables wrote of his 1988 adventure, 'I was more conscious than ever before that I might not come back.' He did, but with fewer toes. His climbing companion Robert Anderson suffered frostbite as well, and the third in the gang, Ed Webster, lost a line of fingers to the knuckle. Harry, all told, was lucky.

Hearing those words, 'Yeah, I made it', I felt a mix of relief, sheer delight, and envy. I looked at Harry lying there on my lap – cold, weak and blind – and despite his exhaustion, his bashed hip and his clearly painful eyes, I thought how lucky he was. It was over for him. He had climbed to this summit, achieved his burning ambition, and could rest content at last, despite his pain. And I knew that for John and myself there was no longer any chance of us following in his footsteps that night, not just because of Harry's current helplessness, but because the winds had picked up, and were blowing furiously.

It seemed an age before finally that night we laid down our heads to rest. John and I slept on oxygen, in the hope of conserving our strength. We shared a single bottle, with a special plastic tubing, Y-shaped, like a wishbone, delivering a trickle of gas from the bottle to two identical 'night' masks – light, transparent things, such as you might find in an ambulance, or an intensive care unit – strapped on with a little strip of elastic over nose and mouth. They are claustrophobic to wear: condensation collects inside them, until they can hold no more, and it floods in icy dribbles down your cheek, collecting in a cold, damp patch on the pillow. But they worked fine, so long as John lay motionless and didn't flinch, and I lay motionless and didn't flinch. It was bitterly cold, even swaddled, as we were, in sleeping bags. If either of us rolled over, from back to side, or side to tummy, in the interminable search for warmth, the wishbone tubing ripped clean from one mask or the other, leaving one of us fumbling in the dark for the ends of the tubes, and the sockets in the masks, so that the two might be reunited.

To say that it was uncomfortable, the three of us sandwiched like sardines in a space designed for two, the cold biting into our bones, the wind howling deafeningly in our ears, and the tent canvas flapping, is an understatement in the extreme. The rhythm Harry and I had established earlier, drink – just a few sips – oxygen, a few more sips, oxygen, continued, albeit at a slower pace, throughout the night; a cough, or a call from Harry's corner and I was up, half out of my sleeping bag, ripping wishbones from masks and stoking the stove for a brew.

One long hour passed, and then another, until the canvas of our tent metamorphosed from black to a muddy shade of mustard, and the night was over. Hoar-frost fell on our sleeping bags, and in our food; steam from the billy swirled about; it was cold, and damp, and the winds battered our tent, buckling its poles. I sat with my back against one of the corner poles, taking hit after hit from gusts, praying they wouldn't snap the pole and my back with it. My guts ached, and my fingers hovered on the verge of numbness; but I could put up with all of this – just about. It was only the noise – the incessant scream of violent winds – that filled me with terror. 'Are you scared?' I asked John, to which he replied, quite calmly, 'No', leaving me wondering how it was that he and I could be made of quite such different stuff.

There was no need for deliberation that morning. We

knew, without having to talk about it, that there was only one thing for us to do, and that was to abandon the tent, the South Col, and our attempt – perhaps our last? – to climb to the summit of Everest, and head down the mountain to the safety of our Camp 2, pitched on a narrow strip of moraine, 4,000 feet below, in a sheltered corner of the Western Cwm.

'Why don't you leave a Sherpa with me?' asked Harry. He could see a little, with his right eye, but the intensity of the harsh ultra-violet light had left its mark and it would be a while before he could see sufficiently to climb. 'We can go down together,' he added, 'maybe this afternoon.'

John ignored him. He was putting on his boots, fighting with the inners and vast plastic outers, laces under more laces and zips. 'I'm going to the New Zealanders,' he said, and was off, a matter of twenty yards or so, to a cluster of small tents across the Col.

He might have flown to another planet – anything beyond the confines of our little domed tent seemed so distant. But he returned, at last, bearing gifts. In one hand he held proudly a luminous yellow pair of crampons – spiky contraptions you fit to your boots and without which no self-respecting mountaineer would dare to cross an icy slope – and in the other, a titchy bottle of ointment for Harry's eyes. He handed it to me. 'This,' I said, as I dropped a single bead into each of his eyes, 'is going to hurt.'

He didn't flinch, just mumbled, 'Leave a Sherpa with me. I'll be fine this afternoon.'

But he knew, I imagine, as I knew, that John would not contemplate such an idea. If anyone was to stay with Harry, sit out this storm until Harry's eyes were better and he could safely descend, it would be him, strong and able, by far the most experienced mountaineer of us all, and the leader. John would stay; Ang Passang and Kami Tchering would go down with me.

It was as if by telepathy – we in our tent, they in theirs – that the Sherpas knew what John's decision would be. Or perhaps they had made up their own minds, for the next minute, they were standing at the door of our tent, scarlet suits buttoned up, crampons on their feet and rucksacks packed, a look of urgency in their eyes.

Hurriedly I hauled on my boots, harness, gloves, more gloves and a hat, and threw anything I thought might be useful into my sack. Then I paused. The thought of abandoning the tent, battered and shabby though it was, for the hurricane outdoors, without Harry, without John, without anyone, indeed, with whom I had previously climbed in the mountains, was a frightening one. 'Are you sure I should go?' I asked John.

'Get on with it.'

'But, John' – I had to know – 'we will come back up?' It was desperate leaving the Col, but more so if I knew that it was to be for the last time, that the expedition was drawing prematurely to its end and that we would be going down not only to Camp 2, but on to Base Camp, Kathmandu and home, if we were to leave the mountain without even having had a chance to make a bid for its summit.

'Yes, now go.'

With that I crawled out of the tent, stood up, and was instantly knocked to my knees by a fierce gust of wind. Ang Passang lifted my rucksack onto my back, Kami Tchering strapped the crampons to my boots. How did they manage it, in such a wind? Their habit of assisting to the point of nannying was annoying and intensely embarrassing at times. But I didn't object – not then. 'Look after yourself,' I cried to John. But he didn't hear. The words were blown from my mouth in a cacophonous whirlwind into Tibet, and the Sherpas and I were alone.

If we could just make it across the rocky plateau of the South Col – eighty yards or so, that was all – to a point at which a rope was fixed securely to the mountain, from there a line of fixed ropes lay continuously all the way down the 4,000 feet of the Lhotse Face to Camp 2, tucked away in that sheltered corner of the Western Cwm. Ang Passang grabbed my hand, Kami Tchering took the other, and together, three little figures in a high and desolate wilderness, we fought our way across the Col, pushing our full weight into the force of the wind almost as if we were wading through a deep, fast-flowing river. We were nearly there; a few more paces and Ang Passang was fighting with mittened hands, clipping himself, and then me, onto the rope. Along a path, part rock, part snow, leading away from the Col towards a distinctive rocky buttress called the Geneva Spur, we followed one rope and then another. The wind blew still more ferociously, seemingly intent on beating us into the mountainside itself, ramming us into the rocks, burying us under the snow, and leaving us there for ever. Only in the brief intervals between gusts could we pick ourselves up from our crouched positions and make a few tentative steps towards the buttress. Ang Passang led, I followed, and behind me was Kami Tchering. My goggles froze over, all but the tiniest window to the left through which I could see only Ang Passang's boots and his footsteps in the snow. I followed them precisely, my mind on nothing else as he led me by the hand, unclipping me from one rope and clipping me securely to the next.

And so we progressed, cold, weary and scared, until we toppled over the crest of the Geneva Spur and onto the snowy slopes of the Lhotse Face, out of the prevailing wind. Down we went, slipping in the deep, freshly fallen snow, over a rocky protrusion, and down some more. Far, far below, we could see, tucked away in a corner of the great white valley that is the Western Cwm, our Camp 2, the tiny blobs we knew to be tents, pitched on the moraine. On we went. An hour or so later I sat slumped in the snow at the door of a small tent pitched on the tiniest snowy ledge, squeezed between icy seracs, about half-way down the Lhotse Face. It was Camp 3, a staging post. 'Let's stop here,' I pleaded. I didn't think I could take another step; my legs were like a rag doll's, and my throat so dry that it felt as if it would split open and never heal. My tank was empty.

'We go on,' commanded Ang Passang.

'Please,' I begged. Here we could melt snow, make a brew; but I knew as I uttered these words that I was fighting a losing battle. The Sherpas' minds were made up. They were climbing in haste, to Camp 2, and then to Base Camp, and their home valleys in the foothills of the high Himalayas. They wanted to breathe thick air, drink cold beer, cuddle their children and their wives. They were finished with the mountain. I had no choice but to stumble on, until, at last, the black blobs of Camp 2 took colour and form, and we were there. Sandy Scott, the expedition doctor, all grey beard and smiley eyes like Father Christmas in his fur-trimmed, scarlet windsuit, walked across the glacier to greet us: 'Please,' he said, holding me in the warmest avuncular hug, 'don't go up to that horrible place again.'

In a moment a tin mug of hot lemon juice was thrust in my hand and I sat down, with joy, on a squashed plastic barrel, in what seemed like heaven. I could stand up and walk about, if I felt like it, in the large, domed, red and white cook tent at Camp 2. At a little over 22,000 feet there was no need for an oxygen mask, and we were safely out of that interminable wind. The place was full of colour: the red of the canvas, a flaming stove, intricately painted, floral Chinese Thermos flasks. There was food everywhere: slabs of cheese, salamis, and giant tins of custard powder and hot chocolate. And there were Nawang the cook, our team mates, Bill Barker, Dave Walsh and Andy Peacock, and, of course, Ang Passang and Kami Tchering.

I watched these two sitting across the way, ploughing into vast plates of rice. Their eyes seemed to be saying, That's it, we're off home, never to return to this god-forsaken place. But they *couldn't* go. Not now. We needed their support. Without them, there would be no chance of John and me retracing our steps back up the hill, as he had promised we would, and once, just once, making a bid for the summit of Everest.

As soon as they had finished eating, they would leave us to go on down the hill. It was the last chance I had to talk to them, so moving my aching body to where they were sitting, I said, 'Don't go home. We need you here. Please, please come back up the mountain when you're rested.'

It was all I could do. They didn't say yes. They nodded, but not with conviction, the expression in their eyes didn't change, and as I waved them off down the hill, I thought I would never see them again.

That night was one of depressing uncertainty. John and Harry didn't make it down from the South Col. They tried, twice, but each time Harry stumbled over his own feet, and together they were forced to turn back. So they were still sitting out a violent, dangerous storm in a small tent on a high plateau where the air's thin, while the rest of us were ensconced safely in a sheltered corner of the Western Cwm. Tomorrow, would Harry be able to see? Would he, with John's help, make his way down to safety? And would his accomplishment quench the whole team's desire for success? The momentum was down the hill, and home. Would the Sherpas change their minds and return to Camp 2? Would John and I be given one more opportunity to make that long-awaited bid for the summit? Or would I be obliged to accept failure and return home, my ambition still only a dream? I asked myself all these questions, and not one could I answer.

Chapter Two

EVEREST WAS my first mountain. The whole adventure began one quiet, routine morning in the office some time in 1987, when I happened upon a half column inch in *The Times*. 'K2,' it said. 'British expedition invites trekkers to ski to Base Camp.'

I could no more have located K2 on a map than I could some remote tribal holding in deepest Swaziland, and for me to think that I might be able to ski to such a place, wherever it was, and keep pace with an 'expedition' displayed a certain arrogance. The sum total of my skiing was a week a year for six successive years on the gentler red runs of the Alps: I had reached that tedious 'intermediate' plateau that most Brits clamber onto (with brute determination, and not a lot of style), and few clamber off, and knew nothing of ski touring, or ski mountaineering, which presumably this expedition would entail.

But there was something about such an adventure that intrigued me all the same, and somehow (precisely *how*, I forget, but being a journalist, albeit on a humble offshoot of the *Financial Times* entitled *Resident Abroad*, might have had something to do with it) I found myself at a press conference thrown at the Ski Club of Great Britain by various members of the expedition keen to muster publicity.

I remember two characters in particular. One, John Barry, a shortish, bullish man, with buckets of charm, who entertained us all with a slide show and a stream of irreverent, bawdy, verging on licentious, but thigh-slapping anecdotes; and the other, Roger Mear, who was altogether a quieter, more serious individual.

'It sounds wonderful,' I said to Roger, 'but £2,500? Well, I don't know . . . unless, well, unless you might consider my coming as a reporter, and, er, not paying, so to speak.' He agreed, without question, as long as I found my own commission with a newspaper and raised my own sponsorship. I rang the editors of several newspapers and countless obscure magazines to be rewarded with no more than a few ifs and maybes. The problem was sponsorship. It was October 1987, the month, or rather day – Black Monday – of the stock-market crash: people, and companies too, were holding tight to any money they still had, and I had not, anyhow, the faintest clue how to set about extracting cash from a multi-billionaire of the most extreme philanthropic tendencies. And so nothing happened. Another distraction entered my life and I forgot about the whole adventure.

Until, in the summer of 1989, the phone rang on another routine morning in the office. 'Would you,' asked a chirpy, distantly familiar voice, 'like to come to Everest, as a journalist?' It was Roger. Even though I had met him only once, at the Ski Club two years previously, I answered instantly, without hesitation, without even thinking, 'I'd love to. Thank you.' And that was that, this time for real. I told my boss and, with remarkable ease, got a commission to write a series of articles for our parent newspaper, the *Financial Times*. And that was how I found myself accompanying an Anglo-American expedition attempting to scale the still unclimbed North East Ridge of Everest, in Tibet.

Monday, 31 July 1989, and I, with Roger, was in Kathmandu, about to embark on what was to be the most cherished journey of my life. For an hour or more the rain had fallen in a perfectly vertical torrent, masking the smell of rotten vegetation that permeated, from the street market below the small, spartan room in the guesthouse in which we sat. As the evening drew to a close the rain stopped, leaving the air clean and cool, but still heavy and laden with moisture.

There were four of us strewn over rickety metal twin beds pushed against two opposite, and colourless, walls, passing round a bottle of duty-free Scotch. Our two companions were from Seattle, Washington State: Kurt Fickeison, a young mathematician finding his way in life as a tree surgeon, and Garry Spear, an ageing hippie, with sun-bleached hair and bristly chin and legs so long they could only belong to an American, who was, in title at least, the leader of the expedition.

Slouched on the bed, drink in hand, listening, all ears, to their conversation, there seemed to be only one thing that these three men had in common, and that was mountains – mountains and more mountains. They shared anecdote after long and painfully detailed anecdote, on ranges, peaks and gullies, sheer faces, glaciers and deep crevasses, rock routes and ice climbs, in every corner of the world: the Alps, the Andes, Alaska, and a strange place called the Karakoram, where, I believe, K2 stands. At last, the conversation turned to Everest.

'What's ABC?' I enquired.

'Advanced Base Camp,' came the answer.

'And how far is it from BC to ABC?'

'Base camp, you mean,' Kurt retorted.

'OK, then, how far is it from Base Camp to ABC?' I was curious to know this, for it was as far as I was likely to be accompanying them. 'Oh,' he said, 'about 4,000 feet.'

'Is that all? That's hardly three times round an athletics track!'

I knew nothing. '4,000 *vertical* feet, dope,' he said. 'Base Camp's at 17,000 feet; ABC's at 21,000 feet.'

I thought about this and asked how many miles it might be between the two; how far would we have to walk, or climb? I was told that it was probably thirteen or fourteen miles, but that, really, he wasn't sure. How odd, I thought. The concept of vertical feet, or 'altitude', and the effects thereof, had not as yet wheedled its way into my brain. I shut up, for fear I might display yet another chasm of ignorance; and they continued, burbling on about this and that, things called karabiners and crampons and 'Jumars', fixed ropes – 11mm ones, and 9mm ones (or were they 'climbing' ropes, not 'fixed'?) – ice pitons, and the problems associated with glacial travel and seracs and crevasses.

'Well,' I contributed helpfully, 'you can jump those.'

'What?'

'Crevasses. You can jump them.'

'If they're tiny,' said Kurt.

'If you can see them,' said Garry.

I paused: 'What do you mean, "*if you can see them*"?'

I learnt about 'snow bridges', and that a crevasse, more often than not, is hidden, sitting silently under a seamless carpet of snow, like a perfect, glacial heffalump trap.

'I've fallen down hundreds of crevasses,' said Garry, nonchalantly, 'but only up to my armpits.'

'Yeah, but if you weren't roped, you'd be dead,' added Kurt. At which I felt panic swirling in my stomach. I knew that sensation; I had had it once before during a flight across the Atlantic when an engine failed and the pilot had been forced to drop fuel, turn the plane round, and go back to Heathrow. For the first time, I wondered what on earth I was doing following these mountaineering lunatics onto the biggest mountain in the world.

The following morning I awoke, bleary-eyed, and stumbled down to breakfast. It was late. The boys were seated around a table piled high with plates of pakoras and local Iceberg beers. Good grief! I thought as, slowly, their words penetrated my thumping head. They're still blathering on about mountains, and ordered a pot of coffee.

Today was shopping day, and the point of this heated discussion was the list: frying pans, pots, stoves and hurricane lamps for Base Camp; picks, pickets, spare crampons and some of that 11mm rope, and, most important, high calorie cashews, dried apricots and local, fake, Nestlé chocolate. It was raining, again; it had hardly stopped since the moment we had arrived. I was told it was the tail end of the monsoon. A bank of cloud hung over our heads like a vast black woolly blanket, as we hopped, umbrellas in hand, through the muddy, puddled streets of the ancient Tamil district of town, collecting items. Kathmandu, it seemed, was a mountaineer's metropolis, which surprised me, for my only previous knowledge of the city had been gathered from stories of brightly coloured temples, prayer wheels, Buddha, and monkeys, little ones hanging underneath their mothers' bellies, told by my two older sisters, who had ventured this way long ago, when I was a little girl in a grey school uniform. Every other store in the street was stocked high with racks of sleeping bags, boots, duvet jackets and drawers full of odd-shaped climbing equipment, all dusty and second-hand, Russian mostly, salvaged from expeditions that had passed this way before us. These shops were intriguing, but not a fraction as intriguing, in my mind, as the dark, smog-filled stores, reeking of heavy-smelling joss-sticks, sandwiched in between. These, to my delight, were packed with cheesecloth, pictures of gods with elephants' heads and several arms printed on delicate rice paper, and intricately carved boxes, soap stone, and cheap silver jewellery with bits of coloured stone stuck on – all things I remember my sisters tipping from their duffel bags, and cluttering their bedrooms with on their return.

We spent ten days shopping, marvelling at the temples, exploring the back streets, sitting on verandahs sipping old yoghurt mixes through a straw, wandering by the river, riding elephants in the park. It was fun, except for the continuing effort of watching every morsel of food and every sip of liquid that passed our lips, for fear of some ghastly bacterial bug, and except for the bureaucratic tedium of customs officials and visas, which tried our patience, and in the end, delayed us longer than we might have liked.

Finally we were ready to hit the road. Our journey was to take us north, across the Kathmandu plain and through the foothills of the Himalayas to Zhangmu on the Nepalese-Tibetan border, and then in a wide loop – north and then east and then south again – to the Rongbuk Glacier that flows from Everest itself, and Base Camp.

We watched, occasionally passing a few loads, as the

Sherpas – six all told – heaved, pushed and pulled tin chests, rucksacks and long, sausage-shaped hold-alls, up a ladder and onto the roof of a rickety old bus held together with bits of wire and the odd length of string. A basket of potatoes, one of fruit, a couple of tethering ropes, and we were off.

'Ka, Ka, Ka, Ka, Ka, Ka, Ka, Ka, Kathmandu . . .' sang our ageing hippie, strumming his guitar on the back seat. I smiled to myself. 'I should have been born a gipsy,' I mused, as we left the city behind and drove through flat open fields and into the hills. The scenery was beautiful: deep valleys and layer upon layer of paddy-field, terraced on every hillside. Everything was a rich, verdant green, and everywhere there were scruffy-looking goats, spilling onto the road, tiny brown-faced children in gangs, or standing alone, bemused, watching us as we passed. The people looked contented, somehow, through the windows of our bus; or perhaps it was just my state of mind, for everything seemed wonderful on that journey, even the rickety, dilapidated vehicle in which we travelled. It had a little light encased in a cylindrical lamp-shade of stained glass that glowed a warm, comforting red, and a glass partition, separating driver and Sherpas in the front from the rest of us rabble, squashed under rucksacks in the back, which was hand-painted, with lilies and a pair of hands cupped in prayer. The Sherpas acted as wing mirrors, standing on the steps and leaning full body out, hanging onto the door with one hand and banging twice on the bonnet with the other when all was clear. They needed to, for the Nepalese drive like the Italians, and their roads are more pot-holed and littered with rubble than any I've seen elsewhere in the world. We were obliged repeatedly to stop, jump out, and heave away great boulders that had fallen on the road from some unseen cliff high above; or else, scramble about in search of loose rubble and rocks to fill holes in the road where water, gushing from the mountain tops, had washed away great chunks of the hillside into the Sun Kosi river, thundering in torrents of froth in a gorge, far below.

'Must be grade six E,' said Lorne, knowingly, peering over the edge of the precipice. Lorne was our twenty-stone, vegetarian Base Camp manager, and an expert on white-water rafting. According to him, this river was about as tricky as they get. Must be, I thought, wondering how anyone got so fat eating greens.

The idea had been that we should drive from Kathmandu to Zhangmu, on the border, in a day. But before long, darkness fell, and in a fit of petulance the driver pulled up the bus, switched off the ignition, jumped out, and screamed: 'I can't see, crazy to drive!' or words to that effect, gesticulating and throwing his arms at poor young Chhwang, the expedition head Sherpa, or sirdar, who clearly thought to the contrary. The driver won. Gathering our belongings we followed him off the bus and into the night.

Immediately beside the road was the most darling tea-house, gas-lamp glowing in the downstairs window. We inched our way tentatively up the wooden steps that curled around the back of the house and through a makeshift door into the warmest, snuggest little nest imaginable. It was all wood, the floor, ceiling and walls, with a tiny landing and four even tinier bedrooms. In one, a gang of Nepalese were playing cards, smoking all the while, like gangsters. We diffused into the remaining three, Roger and the expedition doctor sharing with me. The room contained three bunks, pushed against three of the walls, and in the middle stood a low wooden table. On it, there was a single candle. I lit it, and together we sat cross-legged, our bed quilts wrapped around us up to our ears, and tucked into Chinese bowls of noodles and fried eggs, with chopsticks, that some kind person had ordered for us. Then we lay down, still fully dressed, to sleep. It was raining outside, once again that vertical, gushing rain, splashing off the roof as we lay tucked up inside. A heavenly smell of freshly moistened grass wafted through the open shutters, and I thought how marvellous it was to be working on such an assignment.

We woke early, as dawn was breaking, and splashed our way through the puddles onto the bus to discover that our teahouse was only a ten-minute drive from the border. The bus juddered to a halt just short of the town, at a point where, quite clearly, if it had gone another yard we would all have been killed. In front, where once there had been a road, there was now only a gaping chasm. A landslide of mud and stones had swept the road to the valley floor, and for this season, at least, and probably the next, it must be presumed beyond repair.

We jumped out of the bus and were immediately besieged by a villageful of porters who appeared, as if by magic, from nowhere. There were hundreds of them, adult men and women and a few young boys. They milled inside the bus and over its roof, grabbing the heaviest load they could lay their hands on – a big load meant big money. Only when they had secured a day's work did they squat by the bus, skinny-legged, and wearing sandals, to guard their load and light up a rolled tobacco leaf. I wondered what we would have done without them. There were, literally, hundreds of them and we had – not just on our bus, but on another that followed close behind

– literally, hundreds of bags. I had never imagined that a single expedition could require such a mountain of luggage, and that each bag had to be carried, on the back of a man, woman, or child, along what remained of the road, over the Friendship Bridge and up, through a forest on the hillside, to Zhangmu. We looked up from our now redundant bus at this sizeable trading town in the hills in the middle distance. Behind it was Tibet.

I encountered my first Chinese official, dressed in khaki uniform and cap, at the customs post. It was the first unpleasant experience of my journey. He handed me a plethora of forms, one pile, then another and another – and demanded that I fill in every one. I discovered, not for the first time, as I obeyed his command, that third world bureaucracy and Westerners don't mix. Each form asked increasingly absurd questions about videos, bicycles, sewing machines and so forth, driving me into such a frenzy that I completely lost control and ate three packets of biscuits.

From this point we were at the mercy of the Chinese Mountaineering Association. A Chinese liaison officer and a fluffy-haired, bespectacled Chinese interpreter, who spoke not one word of English, were appointed to keep an official eye on us on the mountain, to provide us with transport to Base Camp and to instruct us, on our journey through Tibet, as to where to stay. It was a shame, for Tibet was wondrous and the journey all too short, and the hotels they selected for us, singularly foul. That first night, in Zhangmu, we had to pay $100 a head for a bowl of cabbage soup and a bed in a prison cell that stank of urine.

Apart from the hotels, it is one of my lasting regrets that we didn't spend longer in Tibet. We all wanted to, if only to have time to acclimatize as we gained the considerable height from Zhangmu, at 7,000 feet, to our Base Camp, at 17,000 feet, but, the Chinese said, 'You lost time in Kathmandu; you make it up now.' So we raced through, tantalized by the scenery, and dissatisfied, in under three days.

The journey led us through an extraordinary landscape of vastness, emptiness and wonder. Barren, undulating hills, washed in soft shades of brown, yellow and gold, stood against a distant snowy ribbon of high Himalayan peaks, and an intense, blue sky. And there was detail in this vastness, all the more precious for its rarity: a flower – mauve, or yellow, shaped like a common garden daisy – hidden between rocks; a yak, shaggy as a Highland cow; a tumbledown monastery perched on an improbable peak; and beautiful people. The Tibetans are wide-eyed and handsome folk, the women dressed in brightly coloured skirts; and they live in villages reminiscent of biblical times, with grasses drying on flat roofs and narrow, winding streets, surrounded by patchwork fields of barley, mustard, and a blue flower I suspected might be lupin.

But this journey, I was shortly to be reminded, was about Everest. In a sudden burst of enthusiasm, Paul Rose, the third Briton on the expedition, leapt into the air: 'Quick, quick, look!' he cried. And there, through a tear in the canvas of our truck, far, far off on the horizon, the mountain stood, proud, white and statuesque, a pyramidal summit standing tall above the cloud. It was a picture that was to be stamped indelibly on my mind, for we would soon be at Base Camp where its magnificent north face would provide a permanent backdrop, and a reminder of the reason we were there. Its mood changed, often. At times, its bulk was masked by a band of wispy cloud, and at other times, in evening light, its snow-white peak was tinged pink.

The Base Camp was set in a barren place; nobody could describe it otherwise. Even when the sun shone, burning hot and blinding, the Base Camp, pitched on a vast, flat expanse of rubble left by the retreating Rongbuk Glacier, was desolate. Nothing lived there by choice, bar a few menacing ravens, and a pack of ugly mongrels, sniffing about the rubbish. The only sound was of the relentless rush of snow-melt off the glacier, like the wind in the trees.

Yet there was an undeniable beauty in its austerity. The colours were sharp and defined, the air was fresh, and Base Camp provided, above all, an uncluttered stage for what proved the most enchanting element of the trip, which made those two months on the Rongbuk Glacier one of the happiest periods of my life: the people. For we were not alone: a team of Spanish was next to our camp; around the corner, some Chileans; across the moraine, about a quarter of a mile, there were Yugoslavs and a small party of Swiss. There were Greeks, who, in their spirited, Mediterranean way, left for home without having put one foot on the mountain: 'I have a wind-surfing school, Paradise Beach, Mykonos,' cried one. 'Just ask for Nikos.' And there were Italians, Japanese, Americans, Bulgarians and French, all with their eyes on the summit.

For me, those two months were an eye-opening time of discovery and learning. When I arrived at Base Camp, I had spent the best part of a fortnight with Roger, Paul, and our American friends, and I had hardly listened to a conversation that wasn't solely about mountains. I was beginning to realize just how all-consuming their obsession was. At Base Camp, as I wandered from tent to tent, dropping in for a cup of coffee here, a bite to eat there, I learnt that this passion for the mountains was not just the prerogative of the few Englishmen and Americans I happened to be travelling with, but one shared by an élite band of mountaineers from every corner of the world. How wonderful, I thought, to feel so passionate about *anything*. And how terrible it must be for their loved ones. A good few, I realized, were prepared to sacrifice everything – stable jobs, time at home with their families, even their lives – in the search to fulfil their desires. Those left behind must worry, for weeks, and often months – there are no telephones in the high Himalayas – whether or not their husbands are still alive.

As for me, the pleasure I took from being in the mountains was far more prosaic. I have always loved Dr Zhivago's line: 'Scratch a Russian and you find a peasant.' That's how I felt. I loved the simplicity: no shops, no exchange of money, no buses or underground to catch. I loved making myself as comfortable as I could with only a rucksack full of possessions; I loved washing my clothes and my hair in the trickle of water that ran through our camp, and I loved walking along the glacier's edge, alone, as free as the air.

Often I would look up into the sky to Everest's summit, and admire its form, perfectly pyramidal, and white; but not once in 1989 did it cross my mind that I would climb it, and I was surprised when I learnt that four French women were on the mountain, who, like their male companions, were intent on climbing to the top. I had always thought women had more sense than to risk throwing away a life for what is, after all, a pointless goal. Nothing is changed or improved by climbing Everest.

This is not to say that I wasn't thoroughly enjoying a little exploration of sorts, at a lower, more comfortable altitude. In London, on Roger's advice, I had bought myself an Ordnance Survey map of Everest. It was the first map of this kind that I had owned, and although for a while I had kept it pristine, crisp and clean, meticulously folded, it was now deliciously soft to the touch, rounded at the corners, worn on the folds, and covered with dotted lines and little crosses marking the routes, and camps, of the various expeditions. I knew and loved every square inch of it, and walked a good deal of what it illustrated in the valleys. From the Base Camp, it showed the Rongbuk Glacier running along the valley floor to the south, towards Everest's north face, at first like a fat snake, until it forks round either side of a peak called Changtse that partly obscures the view of Everest from Base Camp.

The path that our expedition was to take ran up the eastern fork of the glacier, thirteen miles or so to Advanced Base Camp (Kurt was right), at the foot of the North East Ridge. Roger, Paul and the Americans on the team took only this path, for their minds were only on the summit and they had no energy to spare for extraneous frivolities. I, on the other hand, had lots.

I decided one day that I should like to visit the Lho La. The name, I thought, was beautiful. A snowy col, it sits at the head of the western fork of the glacier – the main Rongbuk Glacier, in fact – at the foot of Everest's West Ridge. My map told me it formed the border between Tibet and Nepal, and according to various chit-chat around Base Camp, it was where the Yugoslavs and the Chileans attempting to climb the West Ridge had a camp.

One day, I packed my rucksack and went. I bumped into

a fellow journalist, a Yugoslav called Mimi, along the way. I found him, large and bearded, wrapped up in a bivouac bag in the middle of a desolate stretch of moraine, reading a book. 'It was snowing,' he said. 'Thought I'd have a rest.'

'But it hasn't been snowing for hours!' I rebuked him, dragging him to his feet, and together we ambled on for a couple of blissful days, stopping every hundred yards to break open a bar of chocolate, and chat, until, late on the second evening, head-torches burning, we reached the Yugoslavs' and Chileans' camps juxtaposed on the snow-carpeted glacier by the Lho La.

The Chileans had open house that night, sharing their single pot of stew with me, Mimi and as many of his friends as could be squashed into the tent. The jokes reverberating off the canvas walls wore a bit thin in translation from Spanish, to Yugoslav, to English; but I shall never forget the Chileans – all dressed in expedition yellow – bursting, spontaneously, into their national anthem.

We stood outside for hours that night, in the dry, chilling air, gazing in awe at the glorious cirque of peaks that surrounded us. There was Changtse, and Khumbutse, Lingtren, and, high above our heads, Everest, gleaming white against the night sky. The Chileans pointed out their route leading onto the West Ridge, and at the foot of the ridge, the broad and beautiful snow-covered col of the Lho La. It was to the Lho La that Bullock and Tilman had come long before us, in the early years of this century, to peer down over its edge, reconnoitring the approach to Everest on its southern side, by way of the Khumbu Glacier and Western Cwm.

I woke up next morning determined that I would fulfil

just one goal that I had set myself on the mountain. A couple of weeks ago, I had walked with the team the length of the eastern Rongbuk Glacier to our Advanced Base Camp at its head, at the foot of the North East Ridge. I wanted to return. The goal I had set myself was to climb the 2,000 feet of a steepish incline called Bill's Buttress, to a point atop it on the North East Ridge that, secretly, I had nominated my own summit. It was here that Roger and Paul had established the first camp on the ridge – on the mountain, proper, so to speak – at 23,500 feet.

A few days later I sat, in some discomfort, on a wobbly pile of rocks at Advanced Base Camp. 'They'll think you're mad at home,' muttered Tim Gage, one of our American friends. From where we sat we could study Bill's Buttress with ease. An hour or so's walk away across the upper reaches of the East Rongbuk Glacier, stretched before us in a gently undulating, snowy loveliness, was Everest, glorious in the sunshine. The route to Camp 1, on top of Bill's Buttress, followed a ridge angled at some 40 degrees, on the horizon, straight ahead. Above the buttress, to the right, rose the massive saw-toothed pinnacles which had proved the major obstacle on this unclimbed North East Ridge and ensured, to this day, that it could rightfully retain its reputation. Right again, and there was the summit.

'You'll be on your own, kid,' Tim added. 'Fall sick up there and there'll be no one in any state to help you down.'

'Thanks, Tim,' I retorted, falling into gloom. Only yesterday he had been so encouraging. He had taught me the ropes, literally: how to *jumar* up them, using a friction device, and abseil down, full body-weight leaning from the slope; and how to fall, prostrate, ice-axe to the ground, should some unlucky person tethered to the same rope just happen upon a crevasse.

'I'm trying to help, that's all,' he said. 'You should think about it.'

My fears were two-fold: first, the possibility of an accident – a fall, perhaps, or an avalanche – and second, the onset of a couple of peculiar illnesses of which I knew little. One was pulmonary oedema, in which fluid collects in the lungs, and the other, sounding much nastier, I thought, was cerebral oedema, where fluid would collect in the few remaining cells of grey matter that comprised my brain. Either, I was told, could strike suddenly, and fatally, at high altitude.

I balanced these worries against . . . what? A futile desire to say that I had done it, perhaps? A niggling curiosity to taste something of what drove these seemingly sane men repeatedly to sacrifice jobs and families just to climb? Or simply for something to write about in my next dispatch to the *Financial Times*?

'Are you climbing to Camp 1?'

It was Chhwang, our *sirdar*. He was heading down to Base Camp, packed and ready to go.

'Yeah, I suppose so,' I said.

'You'll need kit?'

'Yes.' I had nothing but a pair of leather walking boots and a ski jacket borrowed off a friend in the office.

He unpacked his perfectly organized pack, digging deep for his harness, plastic boots, crampons and ice-axe, and handed them to me.

'Thanks, Chhwang.'

'I wish I was climbing with you,' he said.

'I wish you were, too.'

It was three or four days before favourable weather conditions coincided with my vacillating will to fulfil my goal. I thought it strange at the time, but there were mornings at this high altitude – 21,000 feet – when no amount of encouragement could have persuaded me to take even one step in the direction of Bill's Buttress. It was the lack of oxygen, I suppose, that leached the energy from my body and brain.

On one particular morning, though, I felt strong. Tim had deserted me, in my weakness, and it was Kurt Fickeison who was on the other end of the rope as I stepped, with a sudden and overwhelming feeling of relief, onto the glacier. It was as if all the preparations over the preceding months, all the weeks spent acclimatizing, all the days procrastinating at Advanced Base Camp, looking thoughtfully at the buttress, were, in a single step, worthwhile.

The glacier was a strange, lovely place. Crunching through the snow – still crisp, at this early hour – we left all hints of human habitation behind us. There were no tents, no clutter, no crowds, only the vast expanse of the glacier that surrounded us completely like a large white sheet, a nothingness, but for long, oblong crevasses that lay, dark and sinister, in the snow.

An hour passed and we were at the foot of the steep incline that led up and onto the ridge to Camp 1, at the foot of Bill's snowy Buttress. It was time to put my climbing lessons into practice. Kurt led, and I followed, clipping onto a fixed rope that marked our route and climbing precisely in his well-trodden footsteps, one deliberate, cramponed step, and then another.

I loved it. It was warm, almost too hot, as the sun rose in the sky and we climbed higher and higher, each step rewarded

with an increasingly bewildering view as one distant Himalayan peak popped up behind another, each gleaming white in
the sunshine. We climbed for four hours in the scorching
heat, gaining perhaps 1,500 feet, but our good fortune wasn't
to last. It began to snow, masking our vision and chilling us
to the bone. What had been an intense pleasure turned, in a
second, to nothing but a test of endurance. The ground was
steep. We had to rest longer with every step, the air now
uncomfortably thin. Snow whipped in our faces, and there
was nothing but a cold, silent greyness, punctuated by the
eerie sound of avalanches rumbling off unseen slopes.

Alone, I have no doubt that the last few hundred feet
would have defeated me. Such was the effort that even twenty
yards from the top, within sight of the small red flag that I
knew marked the site of our camp, hidden just over the brow,
I sat back in my harness and rested for ten minutes, maybe
more. I was exhausted, and certainly would have turned right
round and gone back down, had it not been for Kurt encouraging me to the last.

He raced ahead, just the last few yards, and as – finally –
I collapsed into the tent, there, steaming away, was a brew
waiting for me. The feeling of relief was immeasurable. Our
goal accomplished, we sat for an hour or more, drinking,
eating, and chatting. Even the smallest of pleasures – a cup of
warm, sweet milk, a square of chocolate – seemed the most
exquisite delight. So this, I pondered, is what it is all about.
In one day, I had experienced moments of extreme physical
discomfort, but also moments of wonder.

It took us three hours to rattle down the route that had
taken seven hours to climb. Dusk was just fading into dark as
we tumbled into the cook tent at Advanced Base Camp.

'Just in time for a coffee,' said Paul. He and Roger were winding up the evening after supper.

'I think,' he said, 'you've just been higher than any British woman on Everest.'

'You're joking.'

This I found extraordinarily hard to believe. But they thought about it. Two legendary British climbers, Jo Tasker and Peter Boardman, had been lost in the pinnacles on the North East Ridge, in 1986. Their bereaved women had been here, to Advanced Base Camp; but no British woman, as far as they were aware, had been any higher. Certainly, no British woman had attempted to climb to the summit.

Chapter Three

I<small>T WAS THE</small> romance of Everest that I fell in love with. When we were on the mountain, there were at least two, or even three, hundred people of all different colours, creeds and nationalities, each with an unrelenting desire to stand on the summit. Everest's summit is the highest point in the world, and for some unquantifiable reason people are drawn to it, as they are to the North and South Poles, and the deepest ocean. For me, though, and, I would argue, for Roger and Paul, Everest held a peculiarly special appeal. That autumn of 1989, among all the other climbers, Roger, Paul and I were the only Britons. And Everest is a British mountain. I qualify my statement, for clearly in the most important senses – geographically and politically – it is nothing of the sort. Everest lies in Nepal and in Tibet. It straddles these two countries, and belongs, if a mountain can belong to anyone, to the Nepalese and Tibetan people. However, in the *historical* sense, Everest is British.

Everest takes its name from that of the Surveyor General of India, Sir George Everest. When I was at Base Camp, one clear, crisp night, I looked along the length of the Rongbuk valley to the mountain, standing proud at its head, to the first rock step, and the second, high on the North Ridge just short of the summit, silhouetted against the night sky. A young Mexican turned to me and asked, 'Do you think Mallory and Irvine made it to the top?' And I answered, 'Maybe, but there again maybe not, but really, you know, it doesn't matter because it was first climbed by a British expedition anyhow, led by a British colonel.' Everest's history is British, just as Annapurna's is French, and K2's Italian, and at Base Camp, as one of only three Britons in the crowd, I couldn't help but feel a glow of pride.

I have no idea when I first decided that I wanted to climb Everest, although an acquaintance I made, now a friend, told me only the other day that I said to him at our first meeting, over lunch, shortly after my 1989 trip to Everest, that, one day, I would like to climb it. But if I said that then – which I must have done – it was only a dream, as a small boy might dream of being a racing driver, or an astronaut.

Only one thing was certain after that trip, and that was that I had fallen in love with the mountains. This wasn't anything new, for even when I was a small child, when we spent happy days on farms in the Yorkshire Dales, and on Dartmoor, scrambling over the moors, building dams and swimming in the glorious peaty rivers, I always loved the movement in the hills. I grew up in Kent, on the edge of the North Downs, and always rather resented that the hills on which I played were chalk, and not nice, solid, brown rock, on the surface of which rain could collect and flow down in brooks, rather than soaking into the ground. In my imagination – which was vivid, when I was a child – I would lay a relief map of Dartmoor on my bedroom carpet, and at night, shrink to the size of an ant, and wander the hills. There was one little patch of the moor, over the cattle grid and the humpback bridge to the farm where we collected the milk, that I knew better, and loved more, than our back garden. We escaped there, for a week, maybe two weeks in every year, and my mother says to this day that when I spotted a knoll, or a tor, I would march straight up it – no zig-zags, or ambling from side to side – until I stood on the top, triumphant. I used to cry when we left the moor. So my love for rocks, grassy banks by the water's edge, and the wildness and natural beauty of hills behind hills wasn't new. It had just been lying dormant in the office, and buying flats, in fancy restaurants and fast city living for too long but had now been rekindled, and developed in the bigger hills of the high Himalayas. I realized increasingly, and with a greater passion every day, that those two months I had spent on the Rongbuk Glacier were the happiest, and most fulfilled, of my life. It was an experience totally unparalleled by any other.

My friend was right: I did want to climb Everest, only shortly after my return in 1989 – but it wasn't with this in mind that my holidays, once spent working on a farm in Africa, or bicycling in China, or hang-gliding in Wales, or scuba-diving in the Maldives archipelago (for always, I suppose, I enjoyed adventure), were now spent exclusively in the hills.

The first mountain I climbed to the top was Mont Blanc. It was early summer 1990. I thought it then the highest peak in the whole of Europe, only to discover, safely down again, that there was one higher by almost 3,000 feet in the Caucasus, called Mount Elbrus. Still, it was a load of fun. I climbed it with the Survival Club, which consisted of a bunch of young people – boys, except for me and one other girl –

dressed in Army surplus, with vast rucksacks, bursting at the seams with penknives, altimeters, compasses, special water bottles, squidgy, like hot-water bottles, and all manner of other Boy-Scout-looking gimmicks and gadgets. Leading them was John Barry, the character who had lectured to us so entertainingly three years ago at the Ski Club of Great Britain. He had spent his formative years in the Royal Marines as a commander in the Mountain and Arctic Warfare Cadre, and was Director of the National School for Mountain Activities at Plas y Brenin in Snowdonia for seven years. John had called me at the office after hearing, to his self-confessed astonishment, that this young City journalist, as he saw me, had walked – *somehow* she had walked! – to Everest Base Camp. 'Actually, John,' I corrected him, 'we *drove* to Base Camp, in a truck. I *walked* to Advanced Base Camp, and *climbed* to a camp on the ridge, at 23,500 feet.' John had invited me to go along with the Survival Club.

I learnt all sorts of things on Mont Blanc: about bivouacking in the snow with just a sleeping bag and a Gore-Tex shell; about cooking awful food, all mixed up together in a little tin pot over a camping stove; about climbing roped, six of us in a line, up gullies, over high, expansive glaciers and along ridges; and about jumping off ridges, this way, or the other, to catch a fall should one of those roped topple off – mostly, though, I learnt about that wonderful snowy playground, the Alps. I loved waking early, before the sun was up, and setting off in a little line, head-torches burning, and I loved watching our moon shadows, stretched across the glacier, and I loved the final reward, standing on the mountain's domed summit at break of day, with the whole of Europe, as I thought, stretched before us at our feet.

I climbed one more route with the Survival Club, on Ben Nevis, and then, foolhardy, I went to Kenya. Again, it was John's idea. He had it in mind to climb the Diamond Couloir, an ice route, on the mountain of the country's name. I had had a long-running affair with Kenya: I had spent three or four months in the Aberdares, the Rift Valley and on the coast, and was drawn back, time and again, to its open country and its vast African skies. When he invited me, I said yes without hesitation. He dreamt up the idea on a Wednesday, and booked tickets to fly the following Saturday. I had time, just, to pop in to see a friend whose father, quite by chance, joined us for supper. 'Kenya,' he said. 'Yes, yes, great mountain. I climbed it when I was in the army.'

'Did you? How wonderful!' I enthused.

'Yes, yes, wonderful mountain, wonderful mountain. We didn't climb it to the top, you understand. No, no, we climbed Lenana – was that it? – yes, Point Lenana.'

This, I discovered, is a blip, a mere hillock on the massif, like a nodular growth on a tree trunk.

'Diamond Couloir?' he went on. 'No, no. The Diamond Couloir is, well, hard – hard as diamonds, you could say.'

In a second, I was on the telephone to John. 'What is this?' I cried. 'I've never climbed sheer bloody ice!' To which he answered, 'If you don't trust me, don't come,' and slammed down the phone. Ha! Bloody men! I called a friend of his who I knew was familiar with this route. He laughed. 'Well,' he said, 'you couldn't be going with anyone more experienced.'

We never did climb the Diamond Couloir, and it remains on my list to this day. We climbed a little bit of it – in my case, about fifteen, maybe twenty feet. It was dark. John led the first pitch. It was vertical ice, or so it seemed to me, and I was hanging on like a limpet, ice-axes above my head and the front-points of my crampons stuck a precarious quarter-inch into the ice, when, from above, John shouted down: 'I think we may have pushed this one a bit far.'

It was terrible. I was fighting, and I would have fought on upwards. But my confidence depended entirely on John's, and with these words, I floundered. He lowered me on the rope, and I stood, feet planted in the snow, close to tears. I had failed, and not just myself, but John, for without me he could have climbed it with ease. It was my first failure in the mountains, and I took it badly.

'Hey, it doesn't matter,' he said gently. 'Tomorrow we'll climb the Ice Window and you'll stand on the top and not worry about a thing.'

The Ice Window route, named after an opening in a curtain of ice, a collection of icicles merged as one, hanging in front of a cave high on the mountain, lies almost parallel to the Diamond Couloir, converging with it on the upper Darwin Glacier at the Gate of the Mists, between Kenya's twin peaks, Batian and Nelion. Mount Kenya is littered with a host of these glorious names for all its multitude of peaks, turrets and tarns, and I found myself taking pleasure in this at least. It's a wonderfully complex mountain.

We climbed the Ice Window. It was my first ice climb – with a pair of ice-axes, and front-pointing, and such – and though not as hard as the Couloir, it tested me all the same, on its steeper slopes and on a traverse, across that curtain of ice. I stood on the top and thought how strange it was to have been climbing on ice, on the equator, with lions and elephants and giraffes wandering about below. And John was right: I hadn't worried about a thing.

We climbed Kenya in September 1990, and, looking back, I wonder if then I might have wanted to climb Everest. But I don't think so even though an addiction to the mountains had truly taken hold. Next summer I returned to Africa to climb Kilimanjaro with Lucy Hannah, an old friend. Poor Lucy, she had wanted a holiday and she wasn't so wild about the mountain idea, particularly when, after only a week into Africa, our pockets, we discovered, were running dry. Kilimanjaro is an expensive mountain to climb, and especially so if, as was the case with Lucy and me, you have no interest in climbing the 'Coca-Cola' route. Still, we emptied our money belts (and any other secret stashes) and between us scraped enough Tanzanian shillings and sterling travellers' cheques to buy a ticket. A little gentle persuasion – 'After all, Lucy, this is the reason we came to Africa' – and we went, plumping for a route called Machame where we saw not a soul but ourselves, the obligatory guide, and a porter each. Kilimanjaro stands a little over 19,000 feet, and we stood together on the highest point of its caldera's rim, Lucy so pleased with herself that she suggested we knock off another volcanic peak, Meru, standing behind Arusha, just across the way, perfectly conical but for its summit – askew, like the wind-cone of an oast-house – while we were acclimatized. We did, and the result was that Lucy, too, became a mountain addict.

It was perhaps after Kilimanjaro that a certain conceit set in. I couldn't climb, in the technical sense. I hadn't led hard routes – or any routes at all, come to that. I hadn't mastered the overhang, or scaled a north face, or climbed solo. But repeatedly – on Everest, Mont Blanc, Kenya, and Kilimanjaro – I had escaped the effects of altitude. I puffed, of course, and moved markedly slower than I might on the beach, but never once did I have a serious headache, or feel nauseous, or lose my appetite, which are common ailments of those venturing high. I'm told that whether or not one acclimatizes well is only a matter of luck. It has nothing whatsoever to do with fitness, strength, or stamina. So I take no credit. But I began to think, maybe I'm lucky? Maybe I *could* climb Everest? Perhaps it was around now that I began to nurture that childlike dream to climb the highest mountain in the world.

It dawned on me that, like a drug, my addiction had started with only the tiniest taste of the mountain, but with each climb, it had slowly infiltrated every cell of my body. I didn't talk about it much. I have a rule that you shouldn't tell all and sundry your plans unless you're quite certain that you can carry them through. You look a fool otherwise when you don't. After all, I could hardly climb – I couldn't even coil a rope.

I broached the subject only occasionally, rather tentatively, in company that wouldn't scoff. And one morning I slipped a cheque – for £100 – to a company called Himalayan Kingdoms in the absurd hope that this might secure me a place on the first commercial British Everest expedition that the company was advertising to take place in a couple of years' time, in the autumn of 1993.

I expressed my dream a few times to John. I admired in him an unusual quality for firing people's imaginations, furthering people's horizons, and instilling in them an enthusiasm to attempt what might seem the impossible. He, if anybody, I thought, would be sympathetic.

But he wasn't. Everest held little fascination for John. It bored him. To him it was nothing but a large, snowy blob, a walk, and where, he would ask, is the fun in that? John is a true Alpinist, one of the best. His interest lies in all those areas I didn't know about: hard routes, overhangs, north faces. When I mentioned Everest to him, it fell on deaf ears. Until one day, completely out of the blue, 'I'm going to Everest,' he declared.

'But why?' I quizzed.

Because, he said, it's for charity and because it's with a couple of amateurs who haven't the faintest clue about what they're doing, or words to that effect. It appealed to him. And what's more, he had been invited as leader of the expedition and had a free rein to invite whomever he wished to accompany him.

How this hare-brained scheme had come about proved, as John told it, interesting. Peter Earl was a merchant banker or institutional stockbroker (he was in corporate finance, anyhow) whose company had gone spectacularly bust to the tune of millions. In the aftermath he and his wife went on a trekking holiday in Nepal. It was here, walking in the foothills of the Himalayas, through tiny hamlets and subsistence farmsteads, with no cars, bicycles, televisions, telephones, or electricity, that he realized that perhaps his lot wasn't so bad after all. What's more, he was won over by the toughness and joviality of the people who lived in this poorest region of one of the most impoverished countries in the world, and the way, he said, 'they laughed at the world as a way of life'. He wanted to help. This streak of altruism in him wasn't new. He had run several marathons to raise funds for charity. Nevertheless, anything he had achieved so far would be put in the shade by what he planned to do next. As he stood, at dawn, on a knoll above a town called Namche Bazar, looking at Everest for the first time, peeping over a ridge at the head of the valley, he decided that he would climb it to raise money for Sir Edmund Hillary's Himalayan Trust, a charity which helped the Sherpas and other peoples of the Khumbu region of the Himalayas. He had never climbed, or even spent a night in a tent.

He persuaded the Nepalese government to issue him with official approval to climb Everest only two years from then, in the post-monsoon season of 1993. It would be forty years on from the first ascent of Everest in 1953, and the permit had been allocated for him to climb the mountain by way of the Western Cwm and South East Ridge, the same route climbed by Hillary and Sherpa Tenzing. Thus was the British Fortieth Anniversary Everest Expedition born.

Safely ensconced at home in an Oxfordshire village, Peter called his friend Sandy Scott, the local GP who had been largely responsible, on humanitarian grounds (or was it as a result of a bet?), for persuading Peter, with his wife, and indeed several Shipton-under-Wychwoodians, to take the trekking holiday in the Himalayas. He had counselled Peter, walking through the foothills.

'If someone asked you,' Peter said, 'to be a doctor and a climber on an Everest expedition, would you go?'

'Like a shot,' he replied.

'And what if the climb was to raise money for the Himalayan Trust?'

'Fantastic. Of course I'd go.'

'And what if I told you that I had a permit to lead an Everest expedition in 1993 for the Himalayan Trust?'

The doctor apparently looked closely at Peter, paused momentarily, and said, 'In that case I would say you need to meet my friend John Barry. He's the only climber in Britain who won't think you mad.'

'So, Rebecca,' asked John, 'would you like to come?' Well, what was I supposed to say? Of course I would.

John decided that it might be a diplomatic move to introduce me as the expedition journalist to Peter over lunch. This way he could break it to him that a girl with lots of dreams but no experience whatsoever might be joining him on this crazy venture.

The three of us met at Peter's office in Sloane Street. It was one of those glorious Georgian townhouses with steps leading rather grandly up to a larger than average door, glossed a stern black, just up from Sloane Square. Inside it was all Adam fireplaces, corniced ceilings, and vast, leather-backed chairs, a fitting abode, I was to discover, for its owner, who, at six foot three and three-quarters, was every inch the City gentleman in pin-stripes. He looked a picture standing beside John, who is all of five foot seven, maybe eight if he pulls himself up, and dressed in his best cords and a Benetton T-shirt, bought in Delhi.

We had lunch, and a decision was taken instantly. I would come. The following morning, before anyone could change their mind, I sent to Peter's office my passport number, photograph and climbing curriculum vitae, for what it was worth, to be included on the official permit issued by the Nepalese government to climb Everest. Himalayan Kingdoms was redundant, I supposed, not – I have learnt since – that they had planned on selecting me anyway.

That lunch in December 1991 started a ball rolling that

fast gathered momentum and consumed me for the next two years. John's first task was to select his team. Peter was a fixture, as was Sandy. I had met Sandy only once, in a bar on the Wandsworth Bridge Road. He had impressed me as a dapper sort of fellow with the snowiest white hair. That, really, was all I could remember.

'I think, Bill,' said John. It was typical of him to choose his friends. Why go climbing, he used to ask, without your mates? And I think he's right. It was just lucky that his friends happened to be among the top players in British mountaineering. I knew Bill by repute. He was the Bill of Bill's Buttress. His full name is Bill Barker and he lives in Wales. In the last four years he had been on Everest three times, always in Tibet; only this year, he had made it to within a little less than 1,000 feet of the summit, on his own, and without oxygen – though when I saw him propping up the bar it was hard to imagine this possible.

With Bill came Harry Taylor. The two had climbed together a lot. Harry is one of those extraordinary people who, having hardly set foot on a mountain, one day went to Everest with a Special Forces expedition and climbed higher, and faster, than anyone else on the team – without oxygen. He's a freak, like Reinhold Messner, and became something of a celebrity in mountaineering when he and the New Zealander Russell Brice became the first two men to have climbed successfully through the pinnacles on Everest's North East Ridge, in 1988, and stayed alive to tell the tale. My only encounter with Harry had been at the Royal Geographical Society, listening to this duo relay their story. He was a small grey figure, far below in the auditorium.

There was one thing that Bill and Harry had in common:

neither would climb with supplementary oxygen. 'Well, it doesn't count really, with oxygen, does it?' Bill would say, wryly. And I'd answer, 'No, Bill, not really,' and ignore him. Both men would be joining us, but not, under any circumstances, breathing bottled gas.

Another candidate, Dave Halton, I knew well. I had climbed with him on Ben Nevis, and several times in Wales. He often helped John with the Survival Club. Nothing was too much trouble for Dave, and he was one of two guys, as far as John was concerned, guaranteed a place on the team.

The other was an old rogue by the name of Jan Rowe, one of John's friends from his days in the Marines. He has an energy and a ruthless love of life which is irresistible. I will never forget on Ben Nevis, walking off the back of the hill, the snow deep, the air fresh and sharp, and the sun just dipping over the horizon, turning to Jan, and saying, 'They think me mad at work, you know, all this climbing and stuff.' He stopped in his tracks, and said, 'Yes, Rebecca. But *they're* the ones who are mad,' with the gravitas more usually reserved for the judiciary.

It was a motley crew – a mechanical service engineer, a couple of ex-servicemen, a merchant banker, a handful of whom had climbed, and others who had not. 'Never,' said Bill, grimly, 'have I been on an expedition with so many people who didn't have a clue about what the fuck they were doing.' He was right. Peter and Sandy, in particular, and I hadn't the faintest idea. The three of us, with John as our minder, set off to the Alps for elementary training in the vagaries of ropes and ice-climbing. We stayed with Mike Rhode, a friend of Peter, who owned what seemed to me the most unbelievably opulent chalet in the world. It had touch-button entry, gold taps, a gym, and a ski room with an especially designed little heater with cushioned rods for your ski boots. As well as an entourage of cooks, nannies and French tutors for the kids, of course. It was right bang on the ski slopes in Meribel.

A fresh dollop of snow fell the day we arrived, and climbing came off the agenda. We skied every day, and over a candlelit dinner, or in the Jacuzzi, bubbling hot in the evening air, we occasionally turned our minds to the matter of sponsorship, or permits, or charity balls. Sandy, a glass in hand (it was only this once, sipping champagne in the Jacuzzi, that my social conscience tickled me – a little) suggested that Dr Chris Fenn, a nutritionist, might be invited along, and Peter mentioned a friend of his, Andrew Peacock, who was a respiratory specialist keen to research high-altitude pulmonary oedema. He was keen to come to Everest, in a word.

'And what about trekkers?' asked John. This was his hobby-horse. On every mountain he had climbed and every trip he had ventured on, like the Pied Piper, he had a gang of eager followers in tow. Well, he would argue, they enjoy the trip and I the conversation. It made sense, though not everyone agreed.

It was at this point that Brian, the Australian butler, tiptoed in, and, at Mike's request, turned down the music, just a touch, topped up our glasses, and left. 'What about,' someone said, 'Brian as base camp manager? He's a friendly fellow.'

'And he comes cheap,' said Mike reassuringly, leaving me wondering what 'cheap' meant to a man whose Meribel pad was only one of four such palaces across Europe.

At supper, Mike asked him. 'I'll have to give it some

thought,' Brian replied, 'see what's involved and what I'd be expected to do.' He was wise, as well as friendly.

It was something of a miracle that all of us, gathering from every corner of the British Isles – with Brian and Mike, from Meribel, plus one Paul Deegan, who came along for the ride – collectively jumped on an aeroplane and flew to Anchorage, Alaska. It was a Saturday in May 1992, and our destination was Mount McKinley. At 20,320 feet, McKinley is the highest peak in North America. It lies just a smidgen below the Arctic Circle, and its location together with the altitude makes it, so it's said, the 'coldest mountain in the world'. It was our one serious training trip for Everest.

'I hadn't told my mother about my plan to climb Everest yet. 'Who are you going with?' she enquired, of the McKinley trip, when, the night before we flew to Alaska, I couldn't delay telling her any longer. 'Oh,' I said, 'just a bunch of guys.' My mother is not a worrier – or at least, if she is, she disguises it well. But I was anxious that where Everest was concerned her armour might show a chink. The tactic, I thought, was to delay – keep the sleepless nights to a minimum.

But at work my editor knew. 'It would be nice,' he said nonchalantly to me one day, 'if this mountaineering lark was just a phase and that next month you'll be into baking bread.'

'Thanks, William.'

'How many weeks do you want off?'

'Just three.'

McKinley was one big *Boys' Own* adventure. It was an expedition of vast, American-style trucks, and miniature aeroplanes; of one-horse towns and beer-swilling bars, with moose heads on the walls; and of skiing, sleds in tow, in the wilderness. It was wonderful, in an oddly masculine sort of way. I've never yearned to return. What McKinley was for me, more than anything, was a lesson in what might be called 'sticking it out'.

Crowds of people from every corner of the world were on the mountain. As was the plan, Bill and Harry took themselves off to climb the Cassin Ridge, a strenuous route, by all accounts, while the rest of us, led by John, followed a well-trodden one on the West Buttress, the 'dog run', as it's called. People scampered up and down it all the time. To a Californian it was a weekend in the Lake District. We were confident we couldn't fail.

Only a few days had passed, however, when the cautionary words of Roger Mear, who had passed this way before us, were resounding in my ears. 'Don't be fooled,' he said. 'McKinley isn't a mountain to be underestimated.'

We were stuck in a snowhole at some 14,000 feet, unable to climb higher and unwilling to climb down, forced by a violent storm to abandon our tents and burrow deep, like high-altitude moles, underground. One nameless, numberless day merged into another in an unstructured timelessness, in that northern land where darkness fell only a couple of hours in twenty-four. We were comfortable to begin with, if a little cramped, three of us lying on one side of a snowy shelf on which we cooked our dwindling supply of food, two on the other. But as time wore on it became intolerable. The ceiling of our little home sagged, an inch or two each day, so that sitting upright became an impossibility. It felt like a coffin. Conversation ran dry, word games grew tedious, and what remained of our food became increasingly dull as, day after long, dreary day, the temperature in the big world outdoors refused to shift a degree above $-40°C$, and the winds continued to blow, 80 mph, when the anemometer broke, and more. It was the worst weather recorded on the mountain in thirty years – my lifetime, damn it.

For eight days we sat it out, or maybe it was nine. It was too long, anyhow, for those with commitments at home. Peter, Mike and Brian, in a neighbouring snowhole (we had hardly spoken a word to them during all these days) and Sandy, too, could wait no longer. It was a sad moment to see them go. John, battling in the wind, tethered each one of them to a rope in a little line and, with 'strict instructions, boys, to stick together', sent them on their way. 'Just stood there watching,' he said, 'till they disappeared out of sight.' We could only imagine them retracing our steps, down through one camp, and then another, to a little spot upon a glacier, between the hills, where one of those miniature planes would scoop them up and fly them to Talkeetna. Then, a few beers in Anchorage, and home.

There were just the four of us now: John, Dave, Paul Deegan, and me. That afternoon, the wind dropped and the sun broke through the clouds and shone, warm on our backs as we crawled, blinking, from the snowhole. It was like a midsummer day. 'Should have persuaded them to stay,' muttered John.

Maybe, but it was only a temporary reprieve. The following morning the winds blew again. Would they never stop? An American, a stocky chap, all in red, squeezed himself and his down suit into our cave. 'Heard the news?' he said. 'A Swiss guy, a guide, died in camp last night. Cerebral oedema. And that's not all,' he said. 'Two bodies have been found on the Cassin, and three Koreans fell just here, on the Orient Express. All dead.'

Six people killed.

'Do you know what that makes me think?' said John.

I didn't answer.

'This whole bloody game's a waste of time.'

But my mind was on the Cassin Ridge. Those bodies. Were they our guys, dead?

'It's not Bill and Harry. They're just too experienced.'

John spoke with such certainty that I was almost convinced he must be right. Only a nagging worry lingered. For the first time I harboured doubts about the summit. Spirits were low. This mountain was a killer, and still the wind blew – incessantly for two or maybe three more days, while we lay in our cave. And then, quite suddenly, it stopped.

Just the motion – stretching legs and reaching arms – climbing upwards, pumped energy into our stiffened muscles. We were travelling light now: we had left behind our sleds and carried only rucksacks, making good progress. For an hour or so the sun bore down so fiercely that it seemed impossible that a storm would ever blow up again. But, as I reminded myself, McKinley was a lesson in sticking it out. The mountain threw us its worst once more, forcing us to stop short of our destination and pitch camp on the narrowest of shark-fin crests. We had no choice. The temperature was worryingly low. The wind blew in such violent gusts that it knocked us to our knees. When we finally succeeded in pitching our tent, the poles buckled and the canvas tore. I was terrified. That night I lay awake – the wind was too deafening to sleep – in a silent, lonely panic, petrified that our tent, and us in it, would be blown clean off the ridge to land thousands of feet below on some hideously crevassed valley floor. It had happened once before, I'd been told.

The four of us spent three whole days and nights sandwiched in that tiny tent on the ridge. The wind never dropped, and I don't suppose I slept for a single hour. I felt the strength drain from my body. My morale was low, time was running short, and, niggling constantly in the back of my mind was the knowledge that we had already missed our plane, and that if we delayed another day, I would most probably lose my job.

So our luck very nearly ran out on McKinley. Tomorrow, we said, if the storm is still blowing, we go home. But tomorrow came, and the winds, teasingly, dropped. The weather was far from perfect, but it was fair enough for a summit push.

Four thousand feet – from 16,000 feet, where our tent was pitched, to the mountain's highest point at over 20,000 feet – is a lot to climb in a day, and we felt it. The air was thin, the ambient oxygen, I'm told, about half what it is at sea level. We breathed heavily with every step, stopping frequently to rest, bodies bent, like those of old men, over our ice-axes. Our pace was painfully slow.

'What do you think?' asked Dave. We still had a fair distance to go – exactly how far we didn't know – and it was late in the day, bitterly cold. We dared not take off our gloves for fear of frostbite.

'I'm not turning back now,' said John.

'Nor me.'

McKinley was the first peak that I had climbed against

the odds. We had stuck it out for a couple of weeks, first in that grim little coffin of a snowhole, and worse, in many ways, in a small tent bashed about its insubstantial little frame by the most violent of storms the mountain could throw at it. That evening, though, at about nine o'clock, we stood on the top. The whole of Alaska stretched at our feet in a warm, glowing, golden pink – and there wasn't a whisper of wind.

I sat on the plane home to England, jubilant. It is a strange thing that, armed with success, you forget so quickly all the agony of getting there. McKinley was a confidence booster: it was one in the bag. Scores of punters trotted up and down the 'dog run' every year. I knew that. It wasn't hard. But, by my standards, it had been tough enough in that weather. I don't suppose it impressed the more experienced climbers on our expedition one little bit. Our team cynic, Bill, in particular (who, incidentally, wasn't one of the bodies found on the Cassin Ridge – John was right), had reservations he expressed vociferously, and repeatedly, pint in hand, about the clown contingent on our team, me included.

But on that plane home, I couldn't care a hoot. I was pleased with myself; and, lost in a little world all of my own, I did a few quick calculations in my head. McKinley is just over 20,000 feet. This, so it is said, is equivalent to some 23,000 feet on Everest, because McKinley is at such a northerly latitude and the Himalayas are closer to the equator where the air is thicker. Well, I mused, I could plug into oxygen at 23,000 feet, couldn't I? Or thereabouts?

All of a sudden climbing Everest seemed a possibility. A friend had once told me that success breeds success in the mountains. A climber can happily become used to the idea of scrambling to the top, and grow to expect it. Well, I did then, on the plane flying home to London, if only for a moment.

The truth about McKinley, of course, is that without John's thirty years of experience to draw on, without his planning every step of the way, organizing kit, food and provisions for us, without his guiding us, roped, across the glacier, digging a snowhole, and pitching a tent in that horrific storm, I wouldn't have stood a chance. I think that it was perhaps the realization of our ineptitude – for all of us on the West Buttress with the exception, perhaps, of Dave, were in the same hole-riddled boat – that led John to consider seriously inviting another experienced mountaineer to strengthen the team. It was following McKinley, anyway, that a second Dave – Dave Walsh – joined forces.

Dave Walsh, who is from North Wales which made a contingent of three, with Bill and John, from this corner of the British Isles, is a quiet, modest man with a sense of humour as dry as a parched leaf and a high-altitude record questioned by none. He made the first British ascent of Cho-Oyu in 1988, and three years later, the first British ascent, with Roger Mear, of Nanga Parbat. Both these peaks are over the magical (in mountaineering circles) 8,000 metres, and he had climbed both without oxygen. Doubtless, he would be joining Harry and Bill in attempting to climb Everest without bottled oxygen. The number of players in the team was now nine.

Now, the matter of permits. The allocation of a permit, required by any expedition wishing to climb Everest, and other peaks too, in the Himalayas, is an ever-changing, absurdly convoluted business that would require a Garri

Kasparov or a Nigel Short to untangle. Indeed, not even they would succeed, for it has no logic. Prices change, the number of climbers allowed on each permit changes, the number of permits allocated per season changes at whim. It is a tangled labyrinth of Nepalese bureaucracy, which I was fortunate enough to have nothing to do with.

The permit, along with most of the planning, was Peter and John's terrain. Peter had bought a permit, of course, to climb Everest in the post-monsoon season during the autumn of 1993. The price was $10,000. Everything was fixed. But then, out of the blue, rumours were flying, telephones ringing, faxes whizzing here and there, and the odd snippets spotted in the news pages of various climbing journals. The price, apparently, had changed. A permit was now $50,000 – and was for only five people. If you wanted a sixth person and a seventh person (the maximum number allowed was now seven) that would be another $10,000 apiece. The Nepalese government also restricted the number of expeditions on the mountain to one expedition, per route, per season.

Well, it is just possible to imagine an argument that might have been put forward in this particular committee meeting of Nepalese officials when the decision was made to increase the permit fee so dramatically. They might have decided to reduce the number of expeditions for environmental reasons, because of accumulating litter and so on, or because, somehow, it's just not considered a good thing that a mountain like Everest should be as crowded as it had become. If you reduce the number of expeditions, you reduce the revenue, so you put up the permit fee to compensate. Simple.

What was infuriating, and seemed, to the tidy Western mind, a case of not just shifting the goal-posts, but removing them altogether, was that the new price was being introduced for the post-monsoon season of 1993, and if, by chance, you had already bought a permit for that season at the old price – well, that was tough. Now you pay the new price, please, or you don't go. We had no money, no prospect of any money, and a bill for $60,000 for two fewer climbers than we had planned for. I was worried that the boys might drop me from the team.

What happened next seemed, at first, unconnected with our dilemma. One day, a character called Nick Mason telephoned to ask John if he would like to lead an expedition to Everest that he had planned for the pre-monsoon season in the spring of 1993.

Well, John replied, thank you (he was flattered), but no thank you very much. He explained that he was already leading an expedition to Everest, in the autumn of that year, and that two Everest expeditions in one year was probably a bit much. He concluded the conversation, put down the phone and went out for a run. While he was running, the thought occurred to him that perhaps he should have discussed Nick's proposal with him a little further. When he got back he called Nick, and started a lengthy run of negotiations and deliberations over long, expensive lunches, resulting, rather surprisingly, in Nick Mason not going to Everest at all. What's more, he sold us his permit to climb in the spring of 1993, solving our problem with the Nepalese government. We now had a place for all nine climbers on a permit valid before the new pricing structure came into play. Perfect. The only proviso was that we took on board three of Nick's crew who would have gone with him. There was a Sandy Simpson, who, with the Australian butler, was to be Base Camp manager;

Wyn Jones, a photographer (another North Walesian), and a Noel Bristow (also from North Wales), who was apparently a communications wizard and would be manning a satellite telephone and fax to be installed at Base Camp. I was puzzled by all that: on Everest in 1989 we didn't even have a radio that worked. But this apparatus was, apparently, *de rigueur*, and Peter needed a phone to continue merchant banking from Base Camp.

I was delighted to be going earlier than we'd planned. Secretly I had been harbouring doubts all along about the post-monsoon season. In 1989 it had been during this season that we were on Everest, and once, I thought, was enough. The conditions had been appalling: it had snowed virtually every day, and high on the mountain, the snow, lying thick on the ground, had proved an obstacle through which the climbers couldn't wade. None had made the summit. Yet my prejudice was nonsense, of course. We had been on the Tibetan and not the Nepalese side of the mountain, where the weather pattern is quite different (as if it is possible to tell from the experience of only one year what the weather will be in another, anyway). Pre-monsoon, though, the days would be getting longer, not shorter. I liked that idea. The season would draw to its close only because of the monsoon showers, and this seemed less final somehow than the jet-stream winds that befall the mountain at the end of the post-monsoon season, which usually make climbing impossible. (This might again be nonsense, but these ideas were swimming about in my mind.) These points aside, many more people climbed Everest in the pre-monsoon than post-monsoon season. And it would happen sooner.

Peter and John flew on a jolly to Kathmandu, via Moscow

(Aeroflot tickets being the cheapest) a couple of times to sort out all the bureaucracy surrounding the permits, our kit (some of which, begged and borrowed from previous expeditions, was already stored under lock and key), and a team of Sherpas.

It is difficult to comprehend the amount of planning involved in organizing an expedition of this size. Even the business of acquiring a single item, as it appears deceptively on a kit list, can prove a monstrous, tiresome task. 'Tentage' is a neat little word on paper. Translate this into action and it means supplying a tent to every member of the team at Base Camp, plus tents for the Sherpas, a cook tent, a communal mess tent, and another for storage and satellite phones, more tents for Camp 1 and Camp 2 – here again we needed a communal tent; another for Camp 3 and Camp 4 on the South Col. Then stores are required for each of the camps, and gas; sleeping bags, mats, radios, climbing hardware, rope – and clothes.

Clothes are a problem. There are nine climbers and four guys in the Base Camp support team, plus eight sherpas, all with different inside leg and chest measurements (all believing, fervently, that their legs are two inches longer and their chests two inches broader than they prove to be), and different sizes of feet. Karrimor, the rucksack and clothing manufacturers, understanding the vagaries of the British male, pretty much sorted the problem in one clean sweep by supplying us with huge cardboard boxes bursting at their sellotaped seams with fleece vests, long johns, jackets, and Gore-Tex jackets, in every shape, colour and size. RAB supplied unisize down jackets and salopettes. But feet? Do you plump for plastic boots or the latest and trendiest, highly insulated 'One Sports', which are, of course, only available in Chamonix? And what size do you order when a decision has yet to be made on a single or double layer of sock?

Then there is the oxygen. How many cylinders do you order, and what sort (from a British company, or a Russian company perhaps?), for how many summit bids, by how many individuals? And food? There are twenty people to feed and every bar of chocolate, packet of soup and grain of rice must be carried to the mountain on a porter's back or a yak. There is no corner shop or local takeaway at Base Camp. Then there are air tickets to book, a place to stay in Kathmandu, medical supplies, freight, storage, porterage, and so it goes on.

It was a phenomenal task and I am still wondering how John managed to organize it all, because he did so virtually alone. He had some help, of course. Sandy, naturally, sorted the medical supplies and the oxygen; Peter, being a merchant banker, was in charge of finance; Dr Chris Fenn, the nutritionist, dealt with food, and Dave Halton, the cameras and gismos, at which he excels. But it was John who was in control, and it was a full-time job, even before he launched the multitude of ventures that he, being John, ran alongside.

'What about an artist?' he asked one day. It struck him that it might be nice to have a painting of an Everest expedition, of which you have been a member, hanging at home above the mantelpiece. Lincoln Rowe was invited to join the team. Lincoln might be in *The Guinness Book of Records* if they entered such feats as those he has achieved. He has painted at higher altitudes than any other man or woman alive, at about 23,500 feet on Everest's West Ridge. He had already accompanied a couple of expeditions on

Everest, once in Tibet, and once in Nepal. 'Delighted to come,' he said.

'And what about the Duke of Edinburgh Award Scheme?' said John, and almost before the words were out of his mouth, Paul, who hitched that ride on McKinley, was running around madly putting together what became known as the Duke of Edinburgh Award Himalayan Expedition. A hundred and twenty young Gold Award candidates applied to come along: a 'selection' essay on 'the effects of tourism in Nepal' was set; forty-five essays were written; eighteen candidates were interviewed, and eleven selected for a wet January weekend in North Wales, with Paul and Dave Halton, where the lot of them were dragged up Snowdon. Eight won places to accompany us on the walk-in to Everest's Base Camp, *en route* shinning up a 20,000-foot mountain called Island Peak. The remaining three of the eleven were selected as reserves.

More people meant more tents, climbing kit and clothes, and raising the sponsorship for the Duke of Edinburgh contingent was no mean task. Phones buzzed, letters were scribbled, brochures glued together and money splashed on absurdly lavish lunches, and still, the accounts didn't look good, until, virtually on the day before the youngsters were to fly, the cross-Channel ferry operator Sally Lines stepped in and footed the bill.

The cost of this venture, however – but not to undermine the generosity of Sally Lines – was small fry compared with that of the Everest expedition itself. The total bill was £197,000. Or at least this is what we budgeted in our little red prospectus which was designed to cajole various companies into supporting us. Peak fees and travel came to £30,000; equipment was another £68,000; food cost £5,500

and medicine £2,400; the liaison officer (obligatory) repre-
sented another £2,200; and then, on top of this, were porterage costs, administration costs and so on, and those flights to
Kathmandu and McKinley.

Sponsorship in the form of goods – clothing, food, medi-
cines – proved relatively easy to come by, so that the total
sum of money required was considerably less than the
£200,000 or so initially budgeted. Still, it was *cash* that we
needed: the stuff, as John insisted, that you could pick up and
run through your fingers (he never did get to grips with Peter's
world of high finance).

Had Peter and John not dug deep in their pockets I don't
suppose the expedition would have got off the ground. It is
hard to raise sponsorship, to persuade companies to hand
over their cash, however small a sum, when the country's in
a recession (and, perhaps, even when it's not). Why *should*
they give away their money?

It was, perhaps, my lack of confidence in our commercial
worth that prevented me from raising very much. I tried hard
enough, tapping out letters to a hundred companies I thought
might have even the most tenuous link with Everest, or
mountains, or the big outdoors, or women – anything! But
when it came to the crunch, 'Well, maybe,' they would say.
'What's in it for us?' And I would cry, 'Publicity!' wondering,
even so, how it might benefit their shareholders. I succeeded
in acquiring twenty pairs of goggles and twenty pairs of
sunglasses, from generous companies both, and four Louis
Vuitton bags.

In the end, it came down to contacts, as things usually do.
Peter and John wrote a thousand letters, to firms listed in
Britain, Europe, and the rest of the world. The first dollop of

cash, though, came through a Royal Marines chum of John, Keith Steel, in Edinburgh. He was a director of Glenmorangie, the whisky people. This money was promised but hadn't been forthcoming for what seemed an age, while one month ticked into another and the Glenmorangie contact list grew to include the marketing director Alex Nicol and several people employed by a public relations company called Affinity PIPR Consulting. It was at Affinity's office, in Knightsbridge, that, finally, a meeting was arranged. John couldn't make it.

'You go,' he said to me. 'Just put on your shortest skirt and stun 'em.'

'*Thanks*, John.'

I chose a red, tartan one (it seemed appropriate) and closed a deal for £5,000. It wasn't a fortune, and it wouldn't get a gang of nine up Everest, but it was a start. Still, I was worried. Things at work weren't going quite to plan. William, my editor, knew of my crazy notion to climb Everest. He couldn't help but know because I talked about the mountain incessantly. One Tuesday morning, I remember, I was walking into the office and William asked, 'Good lecture last night?' He's chatty like that. I had been to an evening at the Royal Geographical Society devoted entirely to the world's highest mountain. All the romantic old figures were there, Jack Longland, Lord Hunt, Sir Edmund Hillary, and the younger ones too, Chris Bonington, Doug Scott, Stephen Venables. 'Brilliant,' I replied. 'I was sitting on the edge of my seat.'

'Really?' he mused. He found it hard to understand, I think, how anybody could be so enthused about anything. And I was a little surprised in myself. After the lecture, as I was hovering on the pavement at the doorway of the RGS in Exhibition Road, South Kensington, I saw Sir Edmund, standing there. It was the first time in my entire life that I felt compelled to walk up and shake someone's hand.

So William knew. For months – a year, maybe – we had chatted amiably around the subject without ever mentioning what was blindingly obvious to us both: I couldn't climb Everest in the office. I ignored this frightening truth until three months before we planned to fly. Three months was the period of my notice, either way.

'I've been waiting for this,' said William.

Times were hard. I had deserted them for Everest once before, of course, for ten weeks. And I had an inkling that this one ten-week episode had been considered, perhaps, one ten-week episode too many. Also, there had been six of us on the staff of *Resident Abroad* then. Now, there were three.

'I'll see what I can do,' said William, and wrote the sweetest, most persuasive letter to the publishing director. It would be his decision.

'Well?'

I need not have asked. I had only to look at William's face.

'I'm going to have to go,' I said. The decision took about a femtosecond to make.

'Yes,' he said, 'I know.'

I put on my coat and walked the length of the little grey passage that led from our offices, and sat, in a cold, starkly lit café, for two hours. I was frightened. I had worked on the magazine for six years, and I had never been unemployed. Even so, I had no money, and I had a mortgage. The country was in a recession. Jobs were hard to come by, and freelance journalism didn't appeal one little bit. I had spoken to a friend about this. 'Oh, it's fine,' she breezed, and then, in whispered tones, 'Well, actually, in truth, I've never known it so quiet, but I get by. I have a motorbike. That doesn't take two ha'pennies' worth of fuel, and if I have friends round, well, I give them lentils.'

'But I hate lentils,' I cried, 'and I wasn't born to be poor!' It amused me – a little. Perhaps I could let a room in my flat? It had only one bedroom but I'd be comfortable enough on the sofa. Or perhaps I could let my whole flat and rent a room elsewhere? I could sell my car and buy a bicycle.

Everything seemed horribly uncertain, but I knew I could have made no other decision. We had had a lot of fun on the magazine. It offered security, as well, which I shall never underestimate. What it didn't offer was prospects. Everest, it dawned on me in the cold light of that corner café, had absorbed any ambition I might have had. It had become an obsession, a passion, and I wasn't going to let go of that. I couldn't.

Only one anxiety remained. Three months before we had planned to leave, we still hadn't the funding even to set foot on the plane.

'Peter, I have to know,' I said. 'Are we going to get the money?'

He sat me down, like a teacher with a dispirited child. He said, 'I'm underwriting it.' His company, the Carter Organization in New York, would, if need be, foot the bill.

I handed in my notice, and told Mum. She wasn't in the slightest bit perturbed; or, perhaps, as she was practised by now, she disguised her worries well.

It was the courier firm DHL that, at the eleventh hour, came up with a large chunk of the money we needed. Once again, it was thanks to contacts. John had thought the company slogan, 'Ain't no mountain high enough', fitting, somehow, and – lo and behold – Peter's secretary's ex-boyfriend had once been an employee of the company. They were prepared to listen, at least. The idea was put to its public relations company, Shandwick, one of whose directors, David Fuller, glanced through our little red prospectus and saw John's name. He and John had worked together on a project a couple of years before, in Arctic Norway. We were in.

Peter kept his word. The Carter Organization threw in some money, and so did John, from his own pocket. It was at about this time that I learnt of the Foundation for Sport and the Arts. The Foundation receives over £60 million a year, collected from the proceeds of the football pools, to donate to whoever its trustees see fit. Andy Peacock, our respiratory specialist, dropped them a line and we were granted £15,000.

The last couple of months before we were to fly, on 11 March 1993, were frantic. It's always the way: a deadline looms, and in this respect, and expedition is little different from an article, or a book.

John's workload, it seemed, became intolerable, and as a result, *he* became intolerable. I kept my distance but Brian, the Australian butler, of sterner stuff, jumped on a plane from Meribel and ensconced himself full time within screaming distance of John in the basement of the Everest expedition headquarters in Sloane Street. Peter's secretary, Lou, became almost exclusively the expedition secretary, while the merchant banking offices were temporarily transformed into a depot. Boxes of tents and sleeping bags, ropes, poles and pegs, head-torches, cameras and binoculars, oatcakes, Mars bars, marzipan, and all sorts of highly sophisticated calorie-packed crunch bars spilled into every glorious Georgian corridor, while the boys beavered into the night.

I continued working in the office until the day before we were to leave. Each morning, I would set my alarm early and, dozy, bleary-eyed, attempt to drag myself out of my bed and stumble the hundred yards to my local gym. Sometimes I succeeded; more often, not.

I was concerned about my fitness. I knew, as well as any, that it was the ability to acclimatize, to adapt physiologically to the rarefied air, that was the deciding factor on whether one might, or might not, climb Everest, and that this had little to do with fitness. It might be that Lynford Christie, say, or Sally Gunnell would struggle to make 20,000 feet, while an old codger strolls effortlessly to the top. It seemed reasonable, though, that a certain level of fitness might not go amiss. 'What you want to be doing,' said Bill, wryly, 'is scrambling over hills with a heavy load on your back.' But there were no hills in Fulham. I escaped to Wales or Scotland at the weekends, when I could, and a number of times I considered loading a rucksack full of bricks and walking with it to work. But I never did. I laboured for a quarter of an hour on the exercise bike, and did another quarter of an hour on the step machine – when I could drag myself out of bed – which, John said encouragingly, 'might help on the first couple of days of the walk-in'. As a team, we would be spending the best part of a fortnight walking in the foothills of the Himalayas, up and down, up and down every day, on the near-100-mile journey to Base Camp. That should get my heart ticking over. Meanwhile, I made a point of walking up the escalators in the Underground.

I made several minor expeditions to the doctor's surgery in those last few weeks, for jabs and malaria tablets, and I spent what seemed a disproportionate amount of time ticking off various items on my kit list: crampons, karabiners (four screwgate, four snaplink), slings, hats, gloves and thermals. Sandy, dear man, solved the problem of a pee-bottle. He found one especially designed for women. It was an oddly shaped thing, like a sleeping cat with its head chopped off, a Christmas present.

There were few light moments amid the tension that grew daily as our departure date drew closer. One, though, I will treasure. A year or two on, I found myself once again writing a couple of articles on Everest for the *Financial Times*. 'It would be a good idea,' the editor suggested, 'if the first of the articles [to be delivered before we left] drew some comparisons between the first ascent of Everest, in 1953, and yours, forty years on.' And so, tentatively, after I'd been in contact with his secretary, I telephoned the leader of that first successful expedition, Lord Hunt, at his home in Henley.

'Everest,' he said, very gently. 'Well, it wasn't my favourite mountain, you know.' Those were his opening words. 'And I don't suppose, my dear, it will be yours.'

We met to discuss it a little further in a quiet corner of a coffee room at his club, the House of Lords. Lord Hunt held a place high in my estimation because of Everest. It was he who had made its history British. I'd devoured his book *The Ascent of Everest*, and another, autobiographical account, *Life is Meeting*, with unusual reverence. And when I met this sprightly octogenarian, his liberal views and genuine fascination with other people's lives won me over completely. Such was his unabashed charm that I felt enough at ease to ask,

Might a woman have been invited to climb Everest in 1953? He answered, 'Inconceivable,' and then, on reflection, 'Had there been a girl, she would have been one of us, of course – that would be natural, normal.' But as he explained, in those years immediately succeeding the war, there were few enough men who climbed, and virtually no women, as far as he was aware. Things had been very different then. I had with me a copy of *The Ascent of Everest*, and, before he escaped for a lunch, I asked him if he would sign it. He wrote: 'Good luck,' and 'Mind you make it.'

That was the last civilized moment amid the frenzy of the final few days. Wednesday 10 March, the day before we were to fly, I was wheeled, as the only woman in the team, around the BBC studios, Sky TV, and the Hilton, Park Lane, where DHL threw a highly professional press conference. I zipped back to the office, and then to Sloane Street to stuff a sack full of fleeces, jackets, ice-axe (delivered only that day), and back to the office again, where, with a sweep of the arm, I cleared my desk, bade farewell to colleagues, and tore home to phone friends and Mum, hoover the flat (lodger due tomorrow), water the plants, pay bills, and, finally, pack, for three months, through the night.

On the morning of 11 March, I fell, exhausted, onto the plane. Destination, Kathmandu.

Chapter Four

— ·•· —

WE CAMPED ON our first night in a green meadow on a hillside above the village of Jiri, at the end of the road from Kathmandu. Looking down on its jumble of wooden roofs, dusty streets, little shop fronts, which were no more than kiosks, selling Coca-Cola and biscuits, and a bar of soap, perhaps, Jiri was a tired-looking, scruffy collection of dwellings. But it didn't matter: the high ground above was cool, and the air sweet, and tomorrow we would be on our way, walking through the foothills towards Everest.

There was a fair gathering of us. The climbing team, of course, were there, all but Bill and Harry who would be joining us further along the road, and the Duke of Edinburgh Award youngsters, eight from home and two Indians, who joined us in Kathmandu, plus a collection of wives, friends, friends of friends, including Ione, a buddy of mine, coming for the ride as far as Base Camp. All told, we were a merry band of forty-seven, and that was without the seventy or so porters who would be walking with us every step of the way, carrying our bags, and preparing our meals.

It was evening. In the time it took each one of us to locate a flattish spot, disentangle poles and canvas and pitch a tent, the porters had rigged two long white canvas dining tents, like marquees, with equally long trestle tables, and chairs, and stoked the stoves for supper. Come morning, they woke us, gently, with a cup of tea in bed, and served us a breakfast of porridge, chapatis and huge kettles of milk and tea, at the same trestle tables, in the open now under a clear Himalayan sky, the marquees having been stashed away for the carry to the next evening's camp, and supper.

It was in a light, holiday mood, wearing no more than a T-shirt and a pair of shorts, carrying only the lightest of sacks, that we strolled out of town, through forest and into the open hills. At last, after all those long and difficult months of preparation, we could stretch our legs and breathe deeply the sweetness of the mountain air and feel the sun, warm on our pale-skinned limbs, all in the tranquillity of the Himalayas. I couldn't help but be reminded of the journey we had made in the rickety old bus from Kathmandu to the Tibetan border town of Zhangmu almost four years before, for though the route was different the scenery was just the same. There were the fields, terraced on every hillside, the Alpine-like villages, and far, far away, a thin white ribbon of distant high Himalayan peaks. This time, however, we were on foot, walking along the tiniest footpaths. We could dip a hand in a stream, touch tiny drumstick primulas at our feet and gaze admiringly at the vivid plumages of the unfamiliar birds flitting above our heads.

Day after day, we walked through the hills, passing through one village and then another, each a little further from a road, a bus, or a dilapidated car – or indeed a motorized wheel of any sort, or even a bicycle. The Nepalese, though, despite seemingly being cut off from the rest of the world, must at some time in the distant past have been in cahoots with the Swiss, for their dwellings are just the same. They're chalet-like, with balconies and shutters, slate or wooden roofs, and their mules, like Swiss cattle, wear neck bells.

Every mile or so there was a teahouse, a recent development, I suppose, built for the hordes of passing trekkers on this increasingly popular pilgrimage to Everest Base Camp. At some we would stop for a drink, relax a little and chat, before moving on. I'd walk alone, or with Ione, or with one of the Duke of Edinburgh Award team. 'Do you feel prepared for the mountain?' they would ask. And I would answer, 'Heavens, I've hardly thought about it,' which was true, on the walk through the foothills.

The walk was an adventure that stood alone. Each day, strolling for six, or maybe seven hours, we would enter a fresh land of ever steeper and bewilderingly beautiful hills. We would climb up them, and down again, over rickety wooden suspension bridges slung across rivers in the valleys. And each day we felt a little fitter and a little stronger (and browner), and generally more pleased with our physical selves. It was a holiday for the body, and the best tonic we could have ordered for the spirit.

Often we walked past the people for whom these hills were home. 'Namaste, namaste,' they would cry. 'Good day, good day.' There were children everywhere, smiley faces and tiny bottoms hanging out of the backs of trousers, toddlers suckling mums and little tykes pulling at puppies' legs. I was sitting by a river one day, washing my feet, and turned to see a small child watching me. He reached out a tiny hand, and presented me with a milky magnolia blossom and the deepest scarlet rhododendron flower, both of which had fallen from trees native to the land. He ran away without a word.

The children start work young in Nepal. Some looked no more than seven or eight, carrying loads twice their size up footpaths as steep as staircases. It is a primitive country: a buffalo pulls a single-bladed plough, and a woman, with a child hiding in her skirt, bends double to cultivate the soil by hand. It is rare that you see water running from a tap, rarer still to see electricity, and not once did I spot a chimney.

The dearth of chimneys seemed odd, for the houses were beautifully constructed of stone, with wooden sills, and the ovens were Henry Moore-type masterpieces of aestheticism. They had been moulded and thumbed into lovely shapes, softly rounded at the corners and, like a statue, invited you to reach and touch them, and feel their warmth. But none had a chimney.

It was on the fourth or fifth day of our walk that we climbed over a pass of some 11,000 feet before dropping steeply to the village of Junbesi, and Sherpa land. This was the district of the Solu Khumbu where centuries before, over some long-forgotten feud, the Sherpa people migrated from Tibet. Late in the afternoon, huddled in a smoke-filled tea-house with a young Sherpa and his little sister, I ventured to comment, 'You know, this smoke is a problem,' praying that I wasn't being patronizing. 'It gives you bronchitis.' (It was a recognized health hazard of being Nepalese, our respiratory specialist had informed us.)

'Yes, but no problem for us,' said the boy.

'But it *is*, you die of bronchitis,' I insisted.

He smiled, and his little sister, standing obediently in his shadow, said nothing. She was lovely: she had serene dark eyes and the high, broad cheekbones of her people, and was, we were to learn, the youngest of seven siblings. She had two brothers in New York and another in Italy, married to an Italian girl. The brother bossing her about was off to Germany in the new year to study engineering. They were all well educated, at one of the schools built with the help of Sir Edmund Hillary's Himalayan Trust, no doubt. But it seemed strange, nonetheless, to be holding this conversation with the family cow poking her head into the smoke-filled room. And strange, too, that that night we would pitch a colony of the most technically advanced tents, carried in container barrels of a startling synthetic blue, when all else that our eyes fell on was an earthy hue of brown, or green.

Still, the disparity in our ways of life afforded the doctors opportunity to show off their skills. A couple of nights on we camped in the midst of a small cluster of houses called Bupsa, and a little way off, silhouetted on the very crest of a hill, was a house in which a woman lay sick. The doctors paid a house call.

'Well?' I asked, when they returned.

'She's got mastitis,' said Sandy. He had given her a dose of antibiotics and by the morning, he said, she should be well on the road to recovery. It was so simple – almost a miracle.

It was that same day that we caught our first glimpse of the Dudh Kosi, or 'milk river', that drains the region immediately surrounding Everest. Just after the monsoon it runs in full flood, an opaque, creamy white, as its name suggests, but on this cloudless day in March it flowed a crystal bluey-green. Lincoln captured it with his paintbrush.

From here we would follow the Dudh Kosi northwards,

up and over interlocking spurs close to the river's edge, and along its tributaries to Everest. Bill Barker joined us here, flying into the tiny airstrip at Lukla, and with us, puffed his way up the steep, never-ending hill to Namche Bazar, the main town of the Khumbu, where Peter had been eighteen months before.

As we walked into the hustle and bustle of this little town, my heart lifted. All was colour, noise, and smells. One little corner was jam-packed with shops and market stalls, over-loaded with brightly coloured jumpers, patterned scarves, lapis lazuli, turquoise and joss-sticks. I thought for a moment I must have stumbled through a time zone into the Kensington Market of the seventies. It was all for tourists, of course, and here we spotted them, dressed in walking boots and the obligatory ethnic trousers, picked up *en route* in Kathmandu, or, like us, they were climbers dressed in garish Gore-Tex. It was browsing in this corner of town that I heard my name called, and spun round.

'Keith!'

I couldn't believe it. Standing before me was a man who had been in Tibet with us in 1989, climbing Everest's North Ridge. I remembered him well. Wasn't he climbing with another American called Yan?

'He's here,' he said. 'We're back to try the South East Ridge.'

'Me too!' I said. 'Well, yes, I know I was a journalist then, but I'm a climber now, sort of.'

Others were here too, he explained, a guy called Chuck with a party of still more Americans who had been with us in Tibet. It was as if I had discovered the existence of a rather élite high-altitude club. The same people were on the same circuit, year after year.

It snowed in Namche. The town lies in an amphitheatre of hills, and as I looked down on it, a thin scattering of snow on its roofs and in its narrow streets, it seemed the perfect lithograph, all shades of white and grey. With the snow a stillness fell about town, and rather than rush on, slipping and falling all the way, we decided instead to rest. We shopped for a few provisions we still needed (a couple of ice-saws, some lighters, tape) and spent a quiet afternoon, gorging ourselves on cinnamon buns.

The following morning, I was up early. There was a vantage point above town from where it was possible, on a clear day, to see Everest. This morning, the sky was clear. Shaking Ione awake, I dragged her, Sandy and Andy, the doctors, pulling sweaters over their heads and gloves on their hands, up a snowy path and to the top of the hill. There, in the flat morning light, barring the head of the valley was the vast wall of Nuptse. To the right stood Lhotse, at 27,923 feet a monster and the fourth highest peak in the world. Just behind Nuptse, a mere thumbnail over the ridge, was Everest. We could see just the top couple of thousand feet, if that. It was the view that had inspired Peter to set rolling this whole crazy venture.

It was Saturday, market day in Namche. The sun shone and the snow thawed, dripping off the roofs. The town was packed. Sherpas milled in the shops and in every street, tourists shopped for lapis, jumpers and scarves, and in a secret corner of town, among barrels of rice, grain and yak carcasses, were Tibetans, dark and mysterious. Wild people, with broad Mongolian cheekbones and waxy black hair, plaited and bound in scarlet tassels, and, as I remembered them from our journey in Tibet, with a lump of turquoise and amber threaded through each ear. They came over the high passes from their homeland to trade in Namche. I loved the untamed nature of their dress, and the almost feral look in their eyes, but mostly, I thought, I loved the realization, which I felt on seeing them, that I was at last returning to Everest.

It was with a light heart that I left Namche and trotted, jostling with a caravan of woolly yaks, down one side of the valley and up the other, to Thyangboche Monastery. We could see the monastery a way off, an angular blob amid an otherwise natural landscape with a line of trees, silhouetted in the elbow of a high ridge flung across the axis of the valley.

The original Thyangboche, the one of Hunt's and Hillary's day, had burned down because of a short-circuit in a new hydro-electric plant four years before. It was a pity – the new one, still in the final stages of construction, is painted a rather startling salmon pink and is, I suspect, not as pretty as the original, though doubtless it will weather and fade to a more comfortable shade. Still, the grassy meadow at its front door is the most heavenly campsite in the world. At around 12,000 feet, it is high but not so high that there isn't vegetation, or colour. Yaks graze happily among the tents. And yet, look up, in any direction you care to choose, and there, omnipresent, are the most perfectly glorious snowy peaks. To the north, barring the head of the valley, is Namche, Everest just peeping over its ridge (as we saw from Namche), only closer. And to the north and east stands a mountain whose chiselled icy form, like a giant tooth, puts the Matterhorn into the shade. At 22,494 feet, Ama Dablam is as a child might draw the perfect mountain in a sketchbook.

At Thyangboche we parted ways, Bill, Dave Walsh and Peter heading straight for Everest Base Camp, while the rest of us decided we would rest for a day, and then fork right up the valley, instead of left, with the Duke of Edinburgh Award team, to climb Island Peak.

First, though, a blessing. The Rimpoche, or reincarnated lama, at the monastery had said that he would be happy to do the honour. '*What?*' cried John, when I said casually, in passing, that I thought this a nice idea. 'We're not Buddhist. It's an insult to the Sherpas and, anyhow, it's behaving like some bloody tourist, paying for a blessing,' as we thought we might. But I went. Norbu, the head porter, led a little gang of us to the monastery where at the entrance of a small, sparsely furnished room, he took off his shoes. 'Not you,' he said, as obediently we all stooped to follow suit. 'It is my religion, I must.' We did all the same, a line of us filing in our socks into the bare little room and sitting, silent, on a bench around its walls. At one end sat the Reincarnate, cross-legged and robed in dusty red. He muttered a few words, which Norbu translated. 'He say about Edmund Hillary and great British expeditions and he wish you well.' Finally we were each presented with a biscuit (to eat?) and a length of knotted orange thread to hang around our necks, to protect us from any danger on the mountain. I wore it, treasured it, until its every thread wore thin and it disintegrated. For the little ceremony we each donated 100 rupees.

It was difficult to escape a feeling of history in this place. The Reincarnate had reminded us that John Hunt and his team, forty years before, had been blessed here, and now we were to follow in the footsteps of that pioneering team again, along the Imja valley towards the great South Face of Lhotse, and Island Peak. The peak, at 20,285 feet, had been spotted first by Shipton's party in 1952 on their way to explore the Barun gorge. It was they who had named it Island Peak. It stands alone, needless to say, in a wide basin at the head of the valley. The following year, 1953, it was climbed by a small party of Hunt's men as an acclimatization exercise before they headed for Everest. And now it was to be climbed again by the Duke of Edinburgh Award team and a handful of climbers who, like Hunt's men forty years before, had aspirations to climb the biggest one of all, just round the corner.

We left the monastery, strolling through what might have been an English country park – I envied the lamas. The soil underfoot was frozen, and crisp; snow lay heavily on the branches of the trees, and the sun shone brilliantly, lighting the whole scene and glowing a rich copper through paper-thin bark peeling like snakeskins from the birches. The river splashed in the valley. It was heaven. We ambled on, across the river and high above the tree-line into a heathland of weathered rock, soft, bouncy grass and tiny brooks, like Dartmoor or the mountains in Wales, to a little village called Dingboche, surrounded by a pleasing patchwork of little walled meadows. We camped in one of these at just over 14,000 feet.

Another 1,000 feet, another day, and we were in Chu-khung, a miserable gathering of dwellings that hardly war-ranted a name. The only colour here was in a series of yellow bands of rock, one thick and several thinner ones, stretching more or less horizontally across the vast South Face of Lhotse that stood ahead. Otherwise all was white, black, or grey. I felt sad. It would be a couple of months or so before I saw a tree, or a shrub, or a flower – anything natural with colour.

The landscape became more desolate and colourless with every hour that we drew closer to Island Peak. 'It's like Arizona, with snow on it,' observed Andy. A smidgen of snow lay sparsely over what I supposed must be a form of soil. It resembled a fine, uniform grey sand, or dust, totally lacking in moisture. We pitched camp here in a spot sheltered from the wind behind a hillock and decided, because we had a day in hand, to call it a rest day. Unanimously we designated it Base Camp Island Peak.

I took a leisurely stroll up a bank of lateral moraine and, sitting quietly on the top, I gazed down the other side on a large, frozen lake, hidden in a secret valley. Shadows of clouds passing overhead swept across it, triggering, or so it seemed, the ice to crack and an eerie *boom!* to resound in the silence of the afternoon. How is it, I wondered, that life is sustained in this hostile place? I looked across to the yaks grazing on the hillside. On what? A few parched scraps of lichen? Or moss? In Tibet I had seen a herd of around twenty delicate fawn-coloured deer, perfectly camouflaged against a similarly desolate and rocky scene, feeding, presumably, on the same invisible offerings. And there had been marmots in Tibet, as well, all silky and plump, and flocks of grouse, as here. A brace of Tibetan snow partridge had just trotted by, clucking away.

But at something over 16,000 feet this place was inimical to humans. It was bleak. Strange, then, two days on, and another 3,000 feet up, in air more rarefied still, that the landscape should be so oddly beautiful. We were high on a glacier on the upper reaches of Island Peak, four of us tethered to a rope, at over 19,000 feet and I puffed, forced to stop and catch breath with every step. But the mind can separate pain from beauty when the pain isn't too extreme and the beauty is exceptional. All around lay a pure, gleaming white sweep of snow, broken only by crevasses, lying dark and silent. Around these we trod a twisting path to the foot of a gully leading to a high ridge, and then the summit.

'They're taking their time,' said John. Above us, in the gully, clinging to naked ice, were four figures, Dave Halton in the lead. I was relaxed. Only a couple of hours, I thought, and we'll be standing on the top. We could see the summit, so close, just a few hundred feet above.

And then as quickly as my spirits had lifted, they were crushed. 'There's no rope!' cried Dave.

Damn it. We had assumed, from idle gossip, that a rope had been fixed on this only technical leg of the route. *Now* what should we do? It was late in the day and without a rope it would take a good while for our little gang to climb the gully.

It was John, as leader, who had to decide. Poor man. I had seen him in this position so many times before, eyes distant, searching for an answer. On this occasion, with not just himself, and hardened climbers, but the spirited Duke of Edinburgh Award team in tow, it was especially hard. He so wanted them to stand on top, to 'bag' a summit, to make their Himalayan adventure perfect. But at what price?

The wind picked up a little and a bank of cloud rolled across the sky. 'Every instinct in my body says we should go down,' he said. And that is what we did, just 600 feet from the summit. It was heartbreaking.

The following day we walked back down the hill to Chukhung, and Dingboche, and then turned right up and over a pass into the Khumbu valley, at the head of which stood Everest. I walked with Colette, one of the Duke of Edinburgh Award girls, and she asked, 'Was John upset about Island Peak?'

'Yes, he was, very,' I said.

'He shouldn't have been,' she said. 'It was wonderful, and everyone acted as a real team. I couldn't believe it. I felt terrible and everyone really egged me on.'

I envied her. Everything she said was true. It *was* wonderful, all those glaciers and things, and everyone working together. And it was made more wonderful for the rest of us to be experiencing it with the younger ones for whom everything was so fresh, so bewitching. Her words put me to shame. The part of me that I didn't like very much was manifesting itself again: I had felt wretched in our failure, as I had three years before, on Mount Kenya. And I had allowed myself to dwell on those words spoken by my friend. Success breeds success, he had said. What, I had asked, did this mean for Everest?

On the penultimate day of our trek we pitched camp on a dry lake bed on the edge of a tiny hamlet called Gorak Shep. Looking north, we could see Everest Base Camp. Or at least, we could imagine it where we knew it to be, hidden just from view, at the foot of a lovely snowy col, clearly visible, sweeping in an elegant line from the base of Everest's West Ridge. This snowy saddle was the border of Nepal with Tibet.

It was the Lho La, where almost four years ago I had stood in wonder at the glorious cirque of peaks gleaming against the dark night sky, and where I had listened to the Chileans burst into their national anthem. The mountain, and all that went with it, felt so close.

'Just treat it as a glorified Mont Blanc,' advised Chris Bonington. He was in Gorak Shep, making a film.

'Well, thanks, pal,' I said. 'It's all right for you to say, you've climbed the bloody thing.'

He offered one interesting piece of advice. Having established all the camps in preparation to make a summit bid, he said he had left the mountain, just for a few days, and walked down the valley to Pheriche. Here, at 14,000 feet, he was able to eat and sleep properly, completely recharging his batteries for the summit. It was worth bearing in mind.

We bade him farewell and ambled the last leg of our journey, to Base Camp. It took me by surprise. From all that I had heard, the camp was a shameful dump, a seething mass of human excrement and piles of rotten, evil-smelling rubbish. And yet, here we were in a sort of fairground. Dotted all about were little shrines, each with coloured prayer flags fluttering like bunting in the wind from long ribbons stretched out, as if from a maypole. The tents, too, scattering in little clusters on the glacier, were brightly coloured and cheerful, green, yellow, and red, and right on the edge of camp, instantly recognizable, a vast domed one, a banner stretched across it from end to end. 'The Carter Organization', it read. Peter was here!

'Hi, how are you?' I called.

'OK, OK,' he lied. He was clearly flustered, some trouble

with the telephone I gather. All the crucial bits – the satellite dish, handset and programme – were here, and so was the manual, but without our communication wizard Noel, who was still making his way from Gorak Shep, there was no one smart enough to assemble them and whiz the whole thing into action.

I removed myself from the line of fire and took a wander. Underfoot, in places, there were rocks, some large, some small, and quite a fine gravel sprinkled in a knobbly carpet on the ice. In other places, the dark, underlying, glassy ice lay exposed, and everywhere there were cracks – crevasses in ice – just to remind us that it was continually on the move. All in all, it was a slippery, shifting homestead.

Those who had been here a while had pitched sleeping tents, like tiny satellites, around the large Carter tent in which we would eat and play. We were to do the same, preparing a platform first, laying rocks this way and that, filling holes, making things as comfortable as we could, for this was to be our home for a good few weeks to come, and the landscape around would become familiar. Above our heads to the north was the lovely Lho La, and Tibet; to the west, Pumori, a graceful peak shaped like a well-licked ice-cream cone, and to the east, most significant, a vast and theatrical backdrop to the camp, the Khumbu Icefall, our gateway onto the mountain.

First, though, we had to say goodbye to the Duke of Edinburgh Award team who were leaving us here, turning round and heading back to Gorak Shep, and home. And the trekkers too – wives, friends, and friends of friends – were going too. I would miss them. It had been fun the last three weeks, and now we stood, waving them goodbye. I realized that with them went the last female companionship I would enjoy for a while. The holiday was over. It was time to get down to business, and climb the mountain.

Chapter Five

———•·•———

IF I WERE asked what I thought was the most extraordinary natural phenomenon in the world I would answer, the Khumbu Icefall. It fascinated me. We had been at Base Camp a full day and a half and all this time I had been transfixed by it. Indeed, had I wanted to divert my gaze I couldn't have done, for it is so colossal, so magnificent, that wherever my eyes fell, there it was, omnipresent, an ominous backdrop to our domestic scene. It is, as James Morris reported so succinctly in 1953, a 'tumbled labyrinth'.

From the south side of the mountain there is no escaping it if your aim, as was ours, is to stand in the Western Cwm at its head and to be positioned to climb onto the South Col, and from there to the summit. It is the only staircase, the only doorway, into the Western Cwm, squeezed between the two immense shoulders of Nuptse on its right and the West Ridge of Everest on its left. And it is, unequivocally, terrifying. Like a gigantic waterfall, it cascades over two thousand feet from the lip of the Western Cwm to a point just short of Base Camp at 17,500 feet. Indeed, if the Khumbu Glacier was a river, the Icefall would be a waterfall – a thunderingly huge one of Victoria Falls proportions. But it is ice, and it grinds its way slowly to the valley floor, the great monoliths of ice of which it is formed precariously held in balance . . . until that balance tips, and they crash, erratically, unpredictably, into millions of shimmering splinters.

There is little point in wearing a helmet in the Icefall. If a section collapses while you're in it you're finished. To climb through the Icefall is a game of Russian roulette. I had heard stories of its victims, lost in its gaping crevasses, or crushed in a toppling jumble of ice, and I had thought on leaving London that I might take one look at it, and say, 'Thank you, but not today,' turn round and trot all the way home again without so much as putting a foot on the mountain. And I have no doubt that I had not slept a wink at Base Camp the night before we were to climb through it from fear.

We arrived at Base Camp on Wednesday, 7 April, and on the Thursday, hardly having settled into our new home, we had plans for our first foray through the Icefall. A time was set. We would leave at the crack of dawn at 3 a.m. the following day. By leaving at such an early hour we could make good progress through the Icefall while still in the cool shadow of darkness. We could then drop off a load – a sleeping bag, perhaps, or some food – at a camp at its head in the Western Cwm and rattle back down through the Icefall and home again to Base Camp for lunch.

It was all too quick for me. I felt a need to relax, to tidy my new little house, and sort my kit, and ponder a little longer on the Icefall. But I had little choice. I lay awake through the night, alert as a night watchman, listening to the silence broken by the repeated creaks and groans of the shifting Icefall and the occasional menacing *boom*, like a distant avalanche, as another section of this 'tumbled labyrinth' collapsed. My mind raced. Am I prepared? Have I got my gloves? My harness? My ski poles? I was as an adolescent again, unprepared for an important exam.

But by 2 a.m. I had been listening to snow falling gently on the canvas of my tent for probably a couple of hours. It was warm and, to my eternal relief, as each of us in turn stuck our heads out of our tents into the snowy night, there were muffled cries of 'Back to bed, I think', one after another, and we cancelled our foray for that night and I slept, soundly.

An extra day, and we filled it well, in practising the essential art of 'Jumaring'. (A Jumar, a hand-held mechanical clamp that slides freely up a rope but locks in place when weight is applied, is a handy aid in scampering up a rope fixed to a steep face, or a vertical ice-cliff, perhaps – something we might well encounter in the Icefall.)

'I don't believe this,' cried Bill, in despair. How might it be possible that anybody with a serious intent to climb Everest didn't understand the finer technicalities of the Jumar? But it was true. I don't think Peter (the co-leader) and Andy Peacock had ever used one in their lives. Sandy Scott certainly hadn't, and I had used one only once, on Everest in 1989. With Dave Walsh and John as unbelievably tolerant tutors, we trotted across to a playground near camp of miniature ice pinnacles, shaped like the sails of little dinghies, scurried up them with a Jumar, and abseiled down.

That night I slept soundly, despite the impending two o'clock wake-up call. By three we were on our way. No excuses. The sky was clear. The stars shone bright and the moon was almost full. In single file, John, Bill, Dave Halton, Jan, Sandy, Peter, Andy and I followed Dave Walsh, who had been here once before, along a stony path wiggling alongside the encampment to the foot of the Khumbu Icefall. Here, on a starlit night, we put on our harnesses, strapped crampons to our boots, and walked into the Icefall.

It was easy at first, the ground almost level, undulating just a little up and down. I kept my eyes firmly fixed on Bill's back as we followed a line of fixed rope that marked the route. On the early expeditions, in the fifties, it would have taken weeks to hack ice and cut steps to fix a route through this chaotic jumble, but in 1993, a route was already fixed. It would have been madness for each of the fourteen expeditions that were on the hill to fix fourteen independent and parallel routes, so we collaborated. The Koreans arrived first and they fixed the route. The rest of us handed them some money with which they employed a team of Sherpas to maintain and re-fix the route as required.

Gradually the path steepened, leading us higher and higher, up some hundreds of feet, weaving between, behind and over ice boulders of the most bewildering shapes and infinite range of sizes, into the heart of the Icefall, boulders the size of cars, and houses, and tower blocks! In places they lay protectively, either side of the path, while in other places we had no choice but to inch along the narrowest of icy ridges, a gaping chasm either side, or else, drawing a deep breath, take a bold stride across one, and where it was just too wide, totter gingerly across on an aluminium ladder, laid as a temporary bridge. I was glad that the first ladder I encountered was in the dark. It masked the horror below it. The trick, called Bill, standing patiently on the far side, is to take hold of the two ropes lying as banisters on either side of the ladder, pull back on them, or forward – depending on which way the ladder is sloping – create a counter-force, and then inch across, rung by rung, ensuring each slots snugly between the spikes of your crampons. Some of the ladders were stable, some wobbled and with others the camber sloped alarmingly to one side. Or, where a crevasse had opened wider since a ladder had been laid across it, the ladder hung in the abyss, suspended in space, swaying unnervingly on the scrappy piece of rope to which it was tethered. Some crevasses were such monsters that four, or even five ladders, strapped end to end, were required to reach across them.

There were around forty of these aluminium bridges all told, and I had feared before I had encountered one, that at the first I might collapse in a pathetic heap, burst into tears, unable to control my terror of tripping on one of the rungs and tumbling into the dark, bottomless crevasses that lay beneath them. But, in a strangely macabre way, I enjoyed them. Not once did I think the ladders, or the ropes securing them, might give way. My only concern was that my legs, my clumsy feet or my nerve might fail me. They didn't. Before each one I'd stand and breathe deeply, slowing the adrenalin racing through my limbs and carefully, precisely, step with utter concentration onto the first of the rungs. And as darkness lifted and I could see, if I cared to look, deep into the icy voids beneath, I discovered another trick I could play. Eyes, like a camera lens, can be focused on what you choose. Here my choice was a dark void with all its associated horror or, survival in mind, each individual rung of the ladder. I chose the latter, and the void became merely a smudge.

Despite the months of anxiety and sleepless nights I spent worrying about the Icefall, I found that once I was in it I wasn't scared. I surprised myself. I was being led, almost as if I was an innocent child, into the Great Unknown, a maze of danger, entirely by my own choice, but because others were with me it seemed, somehow, all right. The darkness helped, of course. I entered the maze blind, and by the time dawn broke and I could see, it was too late, we were in the middle of it, past the crucial point of no return. Above all, it was so beautiful that there was no room for fear.

It would be impossible to do justice in words to the exquisite scene that surrounded us as night faded into day. It was surreal – a strange, abstract beauty. A colourwash of the softest blue draped over the surrounding peaks and the precipitous seracs all around us, and the depth and colour and shape of the ice was so rich, so magnificent as to suggest almost a fourth dimension.

Only one steep cliff in the Icefall required us to use our new-found skills in Jumaring. Up it we scampered, several of us on a single rope which was not, I was to discover, a good idea. A jam formed, one of us stuck behind another, and for ten minutes or so I was hanging on the rope with my hands, in a thin pair of gloves, holding the metal of my Jumar against the ice. The feeling in my fingers drifted away and my hands slowly turned numb. At the top of the cliff I hurriedly pulled on my mittens. If you were looking up here from Base Camp, you might imagine, I thought, that this cliff, with the tiny figures, like ants, Jumaring upon it, marked the end of the Icefall. But you would be wrong. We were perhaps two-thirds of the way through, no more, so we climbed on, over, around, between and, disturbingly, under colossal tower blocks of ice until finally we stood at the foot of what, this time, was unquestionably the top. Straining our necks we looked up at a vast ice-cliff, far higher and broader than anything we had seen so far. It was the blunt end of the glacier that lay in the

Western Cwm where, grinding its way down the hill, it met a sudden change in gradient, split, and toppled into the Icefall. It was an awesome sight. At a guess it must have been forty feet high, and just as a tree trunk has concentric circles each of which represents a year's growth, so this had horizontal bands each representing a year's fall of snow. Hoisted against the cliff were two perilously long, banana-shaped ladders, extraordinary things, comprising six, maybe seven standard aluminium ladders apiece, strapped end to end and tethered with long ropes stretched like the points of a star in all directions. We puffed up them, acutely aware that the slice of cliff on which we were climbing might, at any moment, topple with us on it into the Icefall.

Our reward, when we reached the top, was the Western Cwm. I couldn't have believed it was so beautiful. It was a gentle, serene place, in complete contrast to the fierce, jagged beauty of the Icefall. Perhaps it was because we were safely through the most treacherous part of the climb, or perhaps because we had taken one large step closer to our goal – I don't know – but on entering the Western Cwm I felt an overwhelming, explosive joy. The scene was one of such a perfect, gloriously white heaven's gate that even for a second's glance it would have made all those preparatory months of anguish worthwhile. No money could buy this. It was a secret valley revealed only to the few prepared to clamber through the Icefall. Rising steeply to the left and to the right were the West Ridge of Everest, the long crenellated ridge of Nuptse, and, between, a broad and snow-carpeted floor interspersed with at once alluring and intimidating crevasses, around which followed a twisting path to Camp 1.

I stopped only momentarily at the camp before trotting to

the top of a knoll a little further on, close under the Nuptse ridge. I couldn't help myself. From this point I felt sure that I must be able to see along the whole length of the Western Cwm, curving slightly to the left, to the Lhotse Face barring its end. I was right. There, ahead, was the broken-shadowed bulk of the Lhotse Face familiar from so many photographs. In my mind's eye I could almost picture the South Col, which lay hidden from view at the top of it. At that moment, I knew it might be possible to climb to the summit.

We didn't stay long at Camp 1. It was only a staging post for Camp 2, which would be pitched at the far end of the Western Cwm. It comprised three of the smaller domed tents, two of which were stocked high with goodies. We added the contents of our loads and John made an inventory – sleeping bags, gas cylinders, ration packs – while Peter struggled to eat a calorie-packed crunch bar and was sick. The height here was a little over 20,000 feet and the altitude was just beginning to debilitate us, as was the cold. I nursed a little finger, still disturbingly numb from Jumaring up the ice-cliff.

We had arrived at camp just as the early-morning shadows had faded away and the sun hit the canvas of the tents. As we clambered down through the Icefall, around, between and under the icy boulders, over the ladders, the sun had rolled high into the sky. I can't imagine anywhere in the world where the diurnal temperature fluctuations are quite so extreme. The Icefall, comfortably cool on our ascent, was now like a raging furnace, the sun's rays bouncing off the sparkling seracs and sapping the last of my energy. It was sweltering and, after four or maybe five hours, when we finally fell into Base Camp, I was as exhausted as I think I've ever been. Exhausted, and elated. Lying flat on my back on a smooth, weathered slab of rock, I soaked up the sunshine and the pleasing domesticity about us. Harry Taylor had arrived. He sat, slouched in a chair, his music blaring, coffee percolator at his side, as if at this strange place on a high glacier in the Himalayas he was quite at home – which, in a sense, he was, for only a couple of months earlier he had been camped at this same spot, attempting to climb Everest in the winter.

We were a complete team for the first time. We had taken our first step onto the mountain, the sun was shining, an array of the best French cheeses and Italian salamis surrounded us, donated kindly by the delicatessen Justin de Blank (contacts again, Justin was Peter's wife's godfather) and life seemed pretty perfect, but for one niggling anxiety. The little finger on my left hand was still numb. It was also slightly swollen and discoloured – a little paler, I thought, than its fellows.

The following morning I had a shock. What had been my little finger was now an ugly fat sausage, like a balloon, taut and full of liquid from the second knuckle to the tip. 'That was a fucking stupid thing to do,' snapped John. I felt panic well in my stomach. How *could* I have been so careless? So stupid? It was second-degree frostbite.

'Hey, look, it'll be fine,' said Sandy. I sat in his tent, a miserable heap, watching him carefully bandage it up. 'Now take these,' he said, 'and these,' handing me some circulatory drugs and antibiotics.

'And these,' cried Harry. 'They're spare.' And suddenly I was the proud owner of a smart pair of fingered Patagonia gloves.

I wandered back to my tent, to be alone and sulk. I tried to console myself. 'It'll be fine,' the doctor had said. But I couldn't help feeling that even if it did heal it would, surely, be more susceptible a second time. This had happened at 20,000 feet. What would happen at 29,000 feet where it was freezing? And the oxygen levels, and therefore my resistance, were low? Was a finger too high a price to pay for the summit? I pondered for a while and concluded, quite calmly, and to my surprise, for I would never have considered this only a month ago, that *no*, it wasn't too high a price to pay. I could manage without a little finger.

Chapter Six

———•••———

ON 12 APRIL I woke up in the early hours to the clatter of Bill and Dave Halton preparing for a second ascent through the Icefall, and went contentedly back to sleep. I could relax. The plan was that Harry and Dave Walsh would follow them the next day, and the rest of us a few days later. I was happy about this, for I was in no hurry to go back up the hill. I wanted my finger to have a chance to heal and to potter awhile at Base Camp where I knew the routine was gentle. Thanks to an excellent Sherpa team, and an equally excellent Base Camp team, there were few urgencies and little need at Base Camp for us climbers to do anything much.

We had employed Ang Phurba as *sirdar*, or leader of the Sherpas. He was forty or so, quite senior by Sherpa standards, with an enchanting face, like an old walnut, that cracked every time he smiled. He was an Everest veteran, with enormous reserves of experience. He had under him seven younger men whose enthusiasm and willingness to carry loads stunned us all, and also a team of cook boys, three at Base Camp and another who would be ensconced permanently at Camp 2, when established.

At Base Camp we got up as and when we pleased, threw on some comfortable boots and a pair of shorts, perhaps, hopped across the rocks to the mess tent for a mug of tea, hot chocolate, or coffee, and then lounged around waiting for breakfast. It was heaven. If it was warm, which often it was, we might sit and soak up the sunshine, eating one plate of ham and eggs – fried perhaps, or as an omelette – and then another. I never ate eggs at home, but here, because they were special, served only at Base Camp and then only occasionally, they were a luxury.

Food, generally, was a luxury. It wasn't that it was good. It was far from that. It was just that as a normally weight-conscious lass acutely aware of the horror of bulging thighs, in these high hills I could eat and eat and eat, without putting on so much as an ounce. What freedom! I had a reputation for it: 'Could we please have some video footage with Rebecca *not* stuffing her face?' DHL would cry over the satellite phone. But I couldn't see the problem. It was important to eat, wasn't it, to maintain your strength? I grazed all day on marzipan, chocolate and cake. It was marvellous. And in between I'd squeeze in three substantial meals.

Only our nutritionist, Dr Chris Fenn, put a stop to it. Several mornings she would insist that we fast, at least until she had weighed us and stuck little electrodes all over our arms, legs and tummies to measure our percentage body fat. On arrival at Base Camp I had lost half a stone. I was delighted. And my body fat percentage was down to 18 per cent – quite low for a woman, so Chris told me. Some of the men, though, had readings as low as 11 and 12 per cent. It was only John who had arrived a little on the plump side and insisted on removing every item of clothing and his watch, before stepping nude onto the scales. 'They're lying!' he'd yell, and stomp off.

Food, drink and sleep played important roles. And I had a reputation, well deserved, of overdosing on the latter two as well as the first. I had read somewhere that it was essential for anyone who wanted to stay healthy at high altitude to drink at least seven pints a day. Our physiologist confirmed it so I went ahead. And sleep? Well, it was lovely for once to have so much time for it.

There was still time to potter. We all read plenty of books and scribbled letters to loved ones. Peter closed deals on his satellite phone and Wyn snapped happy shots of whisky bottles and watches, Louis Vuitton luggage, and socks, and Jordan's crunchy bars, for the sponsors. The doctors, meanwhile, instructed us on the finer details of bottled oxygen. We must have spent hours screwing and unscrewing masks to regulators and regulators to tanks, and trying, with no avail, to make sense of the calibrations that bore no correlation whatsoever to the litreage of oxygen in the tank. And I spent happy hours stomping up and down the glacier in my One Sport boots. 'Save your feet,' Bill had said of them. They were the best insulation you could buy, and also the heaviest, most colossal and most cumbersome.

It was Sandy Simpson and Brian, our conscientious and ever hard-working Base Camp team, who laboured at the stock-taking and the organizing of load carries through the Icefall. Each camp on the mountain had to be established with tents, sleeping bags, sleeping mats, stoves, gas and food, and it was the Sherpas who carried the bulk of the workload. Three mornings in four they would rise early, conduct a 'Puja', a ceremony in which they burn juniper to protect them from any dangers on the mountain, and climb through the Icefall to Camp 1 or 2, drop a load and be down again for breakfast. These small, robust men carried twice the load and moved twice as quickly as any Westerner I had ever seen on the hill. Their strength and spirit were unquenchable.

I only wish Jan Rowe, John's Royal Marine chum, had been as fit. He seemed to be suffering repeatedly from head-aches, as a result, perhaps, of a recent climbing accident, the doctor thought. But if Jan's body was failing him, his spirit and his love of life were not. Day after day he would stroll down the valley to Gorak Shep, hoping *this* day might be the one on which he returned without a headache, feeling fit.

It was with Jan and John that at 4 a.m. on 16 April I ventured once again towards the Icefall. We intended to climb beyond the first camp this time, to Camp 2 at the head of the Western Cwm, and perhaps on to Camp 3, at some 24,500 feet, pitched half-way up the vast bulk of the Lhotse Face that rose above it. Only at the foot of the Icefall, half an hour's walk from camp, did John discover that he had failed to adjust his crampons. One – the right one, I think – kept falling off, and we didn't have a spanner between us to tighten it. I sensed, from the steely silence, a man quietly fuming. 'I'll turn back,' he said.

He didn't, though. In half an hour, with a twist of a strap, and a bang of a toe, he secured the crampon and we climbed on, twisting and turning through the blocks of ice, and over the skew-whiff ladders. I learnt one lesson in that half-hour, faced with the choice of climbing on with Jan or turning round with John, and that is that I had little enthusiasm for this god-forsaken Icefall. I would happily have turned round. It was only the impetus of others and my innocence that had persuaded me to climb through it once before. And this second time, to my dismay, I was an innocent no more. We set off late. There was no darkness to veil the horror, and my observation of it, once fresh, naïve and unsuspecting, was now only jaded. I no longer marvelled at its surreal beauty and now there was room for fear. Close to the top, where before we had walked a well-trodden path, straining our necks to see an awesome monolith of ice, the path and the monolith no longer existed. The great slab of ice had collapsed and we had no choice but to pick a route across the splinters into which it had shattered, which shifted and wobbled disconcertingly underfoot, serving as a heart-pounding reminder of our vulnerability.

With relief I scaled the last of the ladders and emerged into the Western Cwm. We arrived at Camp 1 just as Dave Walsh, Harry and Bill, togged up like a line of Father Christmases in scarlet, fur-trimmed suits, were heading off along the Western Cwm to Camp 2. Dave Halton would have joined them – he could have done but, frustratingly, he had a cough, and resigned himself to staying with us.

We prepared ourselves, with Jan and John, for a long uncomfortable day, sitting it out in the Western Cwm. It was sweltering. The Cwm, like a vast reflective headlamp, bounced light and heat off its gleaming white walls and snowy floor, and in the midst of it all, in a little domed tent, we baked. We lay sleepily, like four animals in hibernation, fidgeting, all afternoon.

So draining was the heat that I could have lain there all of the next day too if John had not designated it a load-carrying day to Camp 2. We woke early, before the sun, getting out of our sleeping bags and putting on a brew. It took me a while to collect and melt the snow, making tea for John, milk for me, and juice to fill our water bottles. 'Two minutes and I'm off,' declared John, while still I was melting snow, and left.

Oh, well. I would have to walk alone. Jan and Dave would be going nowhere today. I left, a little anxious to be on my own, just as the Cwm filled with light. It felt lonely leaving the shelter of the tent, stepping into this foreign snowy world; but, as so often proves to be the case, once I'd taken the first step the others followed easily in line. I soon discovered, as I had almost four years before in Tibet, that to walk alone is a pleasure all of its own. I was free to take my time, to stop when I pleased, to rest, take a photograph, or, simply, to marvel at the loveliness that lay around me. It was beautiful. I must have stopped every hundred yards, just to look, photograph the scene in my mind, capture it, and with luck hold it in my memory for ever. The path led almost directly along the axis of the broad U-shaped valley that is the Western Cwm, the vast flanks of Everest's West Ridge and Nuptse rising either side. At one point, from high on the West Ridge, an exquisite, perfectly triangular formation of ice fanned glistening to the valley floor.

I felt quite safe. The glacier underfoot was relatively stable. There were only a few crevasses, lovely but menacing in equal parts, to totter across on wobbly ladders, and although I had heard there might be a danger of avalanches tumbling off either flank, if it existed it was minimal. I saw only one avalanche, which had come to rest a few inches from the path.

Also there were people about – always comforting. At one point, my American friends Keith and Yan trotted up behind me, huge sacks on their backs, all loose-limbed and strong.

'Keep going, kid, it's not far,' they cried, pacing by, and I walked a stretch with one of our Sherpas, young Tcheri Zhambu. It was our first introduction. I hadn't had a chance to talk to him before. He was twenty-one, with a sweet smile. He had, he said, been on three or maybe four expeditions before this one. I asked him how high he had been. 'Oh, 7,000 metres,' he said, 'or was it 8,000?' This time, he insisted, he was going to the top. At every ladder we came to, over yet another bottomless crevasse, he insisted on skipping over first, before reaching back, with a smile, and helping me by the hand. And despite his energy, and my slower pace, he refused to leave me to walk alone, until, finally, 'I'm fine, I'll catch you up at Camp 2,' I assured him, and he trotted off, as Sherpas do with quick bouncy steps, a breather, then quick bouncy steps again. It amused me. He couldn't have been more than about five foot two yet he carried a load three times his size, and in seconds had trotted out of view – and the view was long.

I continued on my own. The going was relatively easy – no more, really, than a long, leisurely, levellish saunter. Until the end. Close to the head of the Western Cwm, I could see a line of amorphous blobs, dotted along a strip of moraine tucked under the West Ridge on the left-hand side of the valley, almost at the foot of the great slab of the Lhotse Face that rose above it. It was Camp 2, not far away. But between me and these amorphous blobs was a long, gently inclined hill. I was walking now at some 22,000 feet. The sun was high and the vast headlamp of the Western Cwm was like a huge slow-bake oven. There wasn't a whisper of wind.

During those last few hundred yards I paid for my sluggardly ways in full. I had had my fun. I had also drunk all my drink and stripped off all the clothes I dared, my rucksack now weighing heavy, cutting into my shoulders like a blade. I was in agony, and the burning heat sapped every drop of energy. I wondered if I would be able to carry on, or if I would just stop, here, in my tracks, and frizzle into a small charred heap in the snow. I had no choice, of course, and slowly, slowly, I plodded on, until at last the amorphous blobs took shape, and I stood, exhausted, at the first of the line of tents.

'British camp?' I enquired.

'At the top of the hill,' came the reply. Just my luck! Another couple of hundred yards, another agonizing hour, and I collapsed into camp.

This was the first of my forays to Camp 2. It was brief. I returned to Camp 1 with John the same day to be greeted by the two doctors who had ventured that morning through the Icefall. Jan, with a headache, was still tucked up in a sleeping bag, and Dave Halton had resigned himself to a stint at Base Camp to nurse his cough.

Next day, the plan was to carry another load along the length of the Western Cwm to Camp 2 and return the same day to Camp 1. It depended on the weather, but if in the morning John decided we should go, then go I must. This bothered me: I was tired, my body was screaming, 'Rest day, *please*,' and I knew, or felt I knew, my limitations – my day's excursion had taken it out of me. I should have slept but my conscience nagged. Instead, I lay awake, tossed and turned, and prayed secretly that in the morning there might be a monumental downfall of snow and that, without a fight, a decision would be made that would mean I could rest.

But, come morning, the sky was clear. 'I'm going,' said

John. The Sherpas were carrying double loads again, for Sandy and Andy it would be their first foray to Camp 2, and, as leader, he wanted to be with them.

'Well,' I said, 'I'm not.'

John is an immensely powerful man – both physically and in sheer force of personality, and it took me more strength to resist his will than it might have done to carry a second load the full length of the Western Cwm. I felt dejected, unhappy with the world and with myself. I sat miserably in my little tent until Sandy stuck his head through the door. 'I thought you were going to Camp 2?'

'I was, but John and Andy have gone without me, so I'm not.'

I forgot my misery and guilt. I had a companion with whom to share the day, and a perfectly heavenly day it was. Together, like two contented housewives, we tidied tents, scrubbed billies, aired the beds and checked and counted our supplies. Everything was just shipshape for Andy and John's return. And, most important, I relaxed.

Another day in the Western Cwm, and Jan, still plagued with a thumping headache, resigned himself, reluctantly, to going down. Harry, too, was suffering a little – just a touch of mountain sickness, perhaps – and with Andy, as accompanying doctor, the three of them clambered down through the Icefall, leaving just Sandy and John and me to walk up the hill, along the length of the Western Cwm to Camp 2.

It seemed to me a lot of to-ing and fro-ing, up to Camp 2, back to Camp 1, and Base Camp, up to Camp 1 again, and Camp 2, some this way, some that, hither, thither and yon. And it was. Until Everest I'd thought climbing easy – not physically easy, necessarily, but simple. There was only one aim: to climb to the top. There were no buses to catch, timetables to meet; no finances to juggle, bathrooms to clean, taxmen or editors to appease. No clutter. Each morning on the hill there was nothing to do but wake up, have a bite to eat, pack a sack and climb a little higher than yesterday, until, with luck, you achieved your goal.

Everest put an end to that. Everest, by virtue of its sheer size, makes complicated all things that should be simple. Teams are large: there are a lot of people and a lot of variables. Individuals might feel strong one day, exhausted the next, as already I had experienced. It was just as well, I thought, that not all of us felt lousy in unison, or we'd get nowhere.

This particular day I felt strong. It was a great boost too to have taken this particular path along the Western Cwm before, and in a matter of only a few hours the three of us, with Bill and Dave Walsh, were safely ensconced at Camp 2. Here, in tents pitched on a dull strip of moraine, we would stay a few days. It was in a marvellous position. At a little over 22,000 feet, tucked under the West Ridge of Everest at the head of the Western Cwm, the great slab of Lhotse rising above our heads, I felt, for the first time, that I had stepped indubitably onto the mountain itself. It was one hell of a long walk back to Base Camp, and looking up at that great slab of Lhotse, we could pick out the route we were to follow up its Face and across to the South Col, just hidden from view. With sharp eyes we could see the line of fixed rope, like the faintest hairline crack, leading up the Face one side of a mass of dappled shadows, each one a snowy serac. If we looked even more carefully, between the shadows there were tiny

Above Base Camp (17,500 feet) at the foot of the Khumbu Icefall.

Below Guests at dinner at Base Camp: *centre*, with sunglasses, Alan Hughes; *left*, with beard, Jim Curran; film-makers both.

High-altitude engineering: climbers negotiate the last (and biggest) step in the Icefall, not far short of Camp 1.

Below The entrance of the Western Cwm: the most beautiful place on the mountain, and surely one of Earth's great vistas.

The B team prepare to leave Camp 2 for the Lhotse Face and Camp 3 on the first summit attempt. *From left:* Bill Barker, Dave Walsh, Harry Taylor and Dave Halton.

Camp 2 (22,000 feet), and the Lhotse Face behind.

A view towards Everest South Summit from high on the Lhotse Face.

Above Harry Taylor and John Barry at the South Col, the evening before Harry left for the summit.

Below High life: Camp 4 on the South Col at 26,000 feet. Note the storm-flattened tents and detritus of forty years of mountaineering.

Right Harry Taylor being helped into Camp 2 after his epic ascent.

Above Our tents at Camp 4: frail but sufficient shelter in a desolate place

Right Ang Passang.

Above Kami Tchering and myself on top of the world.

Top John Barry and Sandy Scott watch and wait at Camp 2 over a beer.

Bottom Left Early morning on the South East Ridge. Ang Passang (ahead) and Kami Tchering break trail at c. 27,500 feet.

Bottom Right The South East (Summit) Ridge of Everest. This historic shot was taken on the first ascent in 1953. The footsteps of Hillary and Tenzing can be seen clearly on the ridge crest. (*From the RGS Library*)

Home from the hill: Kami Tchering, myself (*centre*) and Ang Passang cross the South Col to Camp 4 after our ascent.

Tcheri Zhambu greets us on our return to the South Col.

Victory smiles: Kami Tchering (*left*) and Ang Passang back in Base Camp after that climb: two 'very parfit gentil knights'.

black specks, like pinpricks in the snow. Each was a tent. It was our Camp 3, perched upon a snowy ledge, a little over half-way up the Lhotse Face.

On the first successful ascent of this mountain, in 1953, John Hunt and his team had called this Camp 2 their advanced Base Camp. And in a sense that is exactly what it was. It was from here, tucked in a sheltered corner of the Western Cwm, that we would climb on to Camp 3 and Camp 4 on the South Col, and to here that we would scurry back should there be bad weather. As at Base Camp, we planned to stay several days, maybe weeks, and the camp was kitted out with a mess tent and several smaller tents, so that we could stay here in relative comfort. It was Base Camp in miniature. Fewer people were here at a time, and because of this and also because each tent, sleeping bag, cooker, canister of fuel and stash of food was another load to be carried through the Icefall, we economized. At Base Camp we each had a small domed tent. Here we had one between two or three and, in one case, four. At Base Camp we had a tent for cooking, another for eating and yet another for the satellite telephone and radio. Here we had one for the lot (minus the telephone!).

Permanently ensconced in this communal tent was Nawang, a cook. Camp 2, to this at once diligent and delightful man, was home. He had been here twice before, with different expeditions, once for thirty days and once for thirty-five days, on the trot. The moment that he arrived he gathered a heap of flattish-looking rocks with which he built a platform in the middle of the tent. On this he placed his primus stove, pots, pans, and the odd ladle, and from that moment on did what he liked to do best: he cooked. Rice, more often than not, was the order of the day, or pasta or, on extremely rare occasions, potatoes, carried in a congealed, parboiled lump from Base Camp. This he served with grey-looking sausages or tinned fish, or some sort of unidentifiable stew tipped from a little silver bag.

The Sherpas would join us for supper if they liked the look of Nawang's offerings, which was rare, and not if they didn't, which was often. More usually, they would sit quietly watching us until we had finished eating, Nawang had done the dishes, and they could move into the kitchen. They were a joy to watch: a perfect team, one kept an eye on the rice, while another, digging around in his bag, would sprinkle exotic-smelling spices into a stew, and another, perhaps, sitting cross-legged, would roll little chunks of meat or fish into parcels of dough called *momos*.

We passed the evenings perched uncomfortably on a container barrel, or rock, or a cold, empty space on the floor, all of us crowded in our common room. 'How high have you been?' I asked Kami Tchering, one night.

'Twice to South Summit with Koreans,' he said.

'This time you climb to the top, with me?'

'Yes, yes,' he said. 'And with Ang Passang.'

Kami Tchering and Ang Passang were inseparable, like brothers. They joked, laughed and carried loads together, ate together, and shared a tent. They had grown up together and with their young families were still neighbours in the little village of Pangboche, just a couple of days' walk from Base Camp. We spent two, or maybe three days at Camp 2. Bill and Dave Walsh, typically, one step ahead, carried a load one day up the Lhotse Face to Camp 3, and every day the Sherpas went down the Western Cwm to Camp 1 and all the way back up again with heavy loads, in time for breakfast. John, Sandy and I were on rest time. I might sleep, read a book or, if the mood took me, write a letter or scribble an odd note in my diary. I sat for hours with Nawang in the cook tent, eating and drinking – a bar of chocolate, or a slice of cheese – to keep up my strength. In the mornings, with the Sherpas just back from their day's work, I sometimes unloaded their sacks and sorted the contents – biscuits, soups, Mars bars, crunchy bars, more cheese, and salamis – into individual plastic bags, and if I was by the radio while I was doing this, I answered the odd crackly call.

Often it would be from Peter, at Base Camp. 'Just been on the phone to DHL,' he said, on one such call. They were displeased, apparently, that every inch of video tape we had sent them, as dutiful sponsees, showed either me, eating, *again*, or John swearing like a trooper! Could we *please* do something about it?

John wasn't amused. He was feeling rotten with a tummy bug. Sickness was a problem at Camp 2: it didn't seem to make any difference how long Nawang boiled the water or how well he charred the food, infection spread. The next day I had a bout of diarrhoea that continued on and off for the duration of the trip.

Rested, though not entirely well, on the morning of 21 April, I set off behind Bill and Dave, Sandy, and then John, on my first climb up the great slab of the Lhotse Face, to Camp 3. At some 24,500 feet, it would be a good thousand feet higher than I had ever been. It felt good to be breaking fresh tracks again, and for the first part, at least – to my relief – it was relatively easy on both lungs and legs. With a gentle zig and a zag across the head of the snowy glacier that carpeted the floor of the Western Cwm, an hour and a half later, we were standing at the foot of the Lhotse Face. Above us, its great bulk loomed ominously. It was here that we clipped into the first of the fixed ropes that led up its steep face to the camp, and here that the hard work began. 'You go first,' suggested John. He thought I might feel more secure with someone behind me, and he was right. In front of my nose was a solid face of diamond-hard glacial ice. If I looked closely I could see little pockets, boot-sized, kicked by passing traffic before us, which I followed. Pulling on my Jumar, I kicked my crampons into the first pocket, and then the next, slowly inching my way up, John following effortlessly like a mountain goat.

There were just a couple of steep pitches, and then it eased a little – ice turned to snow, and the gradient became a little gentler. Strange, the tricks that eyes can play. From a distance some routes look easy. Stick your nose to them and they're terrifyingly hard. Others look vertical, and yet they are hardly off the horizontal. This one was somewhere in the middle. It looked pretty steep viewed from Camp 2, but was only so in parts, while in other areas it was probably 30 degrees.

It wasn't particularly hard in any technical way. It was just one very long puff. At 23,000 feet, approaching 24,000 feet, the air is thin, the oxygen level low, hardly enough to fuel the body. Slowly, one step, two or three, perhaps, and a rest, we climbed on. Lethargy clogged every cell of my body, so that I could hardly be bothered to move.

Bill and Dave were well ahead, out of sight, and Sandy was so far ahead, indeed, that he was already on his way down. He hurtled down the ropes and fell, literally, on top of us, as I was wriggling a water bottle from the top pocket of John's sack. 'Jeez, you've done well,' I cried.

He could barely talk. He was all over the place, stumbling with his words as well as his body. 'I fell asleep on the ropes,' he mumbled, 'twice.' Still, he had made it, and I was beginning to wonder if I would.

On we climbed, meeting first Dave, and then Bill, descending. 'It's about an hour to camp from here,' Dave said. 'And you don't want to sleep there overnight, if you can help it,' added Bill. What should we do? It was getting so late that the judicious thing might have been to stop right there, turn round, and go back. But I couldn't. The camp was so close. So I said, 'Let's go on.'

Dave was right. It probably took an hour or so to camp, but it was only a matter of minutes before we climbed over the crest of an icy bulge. There, ahead of us, we saw the first of a line of tents. I vomited – I was totally exhausted.

John, thankfully, had raced ahead at this point. By the time I had unstrapped my crampons, collapsed to my knees, and rolled ungracefully into our little tent (perched precariously on the tiniest of snowy ledges), John had a brew already on the boil. 'How are you feeling?' he said. 'Fine,' the reply. And I was, just so long as I didn't have to take another step up that bloody hill.

It took us eight hours to climb to Camp 3, an hour and a half to climb down. Standing in wait outside the cook tent were the Sherpas. Nawang thrust a mug of hot lemon juice in my hand. Tcheri Zhambu unstrapped the crampons from my boots, and someone else unbuckled my harness while I just stood there, all a jumble of emotion. Here was I, playing at carrying a load to Camp 3, and here were they, who did it all the time, waiting patiently for me, and looking after me on my return. It was touching, humbling – and not a little embarrassing. 'Really, guys, I *can* unstrap my own crampons.' And mixed in with all this was complete exhaustion – and overwhelming joy. Despite my snail's pace, we had achieved the day's goal.

It was time for a rest. Next day Dave Walsh and Bill, John, Sandy and I waved Nawang goodbye, sauntered down the Western Cwm, and on, down through the Icefall, to Base Camp. I didn't have a care in the world that night. The air was like molasses, and spirits were high. A bottle of Glenmorangie, or two, or three, and a new day was upon us.

Chapter Seven

———•✦•———

I HAD TWO fears on Everest: one, which I already knew, was the terrifying Icefall; and the other, yet unexplored, was the unquantifiable danger lurking above the South Col, on the last day's journey on the hill. This final few thousand feet, Reinhold Messner called the death zone, for here the air is so thin that there is insufficient oxygen to drive the body. Here, you could die for no other reason than being too high.

At Base Camp we had had some disturbing news: two people who had ventured recently up there had not returned. I lay in my tent, an unopened book at my side, and my diary abandoned. 'Would you like to hear the latest on the Nepali woman?' It was Sandy Simpson, outside my tent. The woman's name was Mrs Pasang Lhamu Sherpa and a couple of days ago she had become the first woman of her country to stand on the summit of Everest. 'She was last spotted on the South Summit at ten o'clock this morning,' said Sandy. These words verified what we all feared and, if we paused for a moment, knew to be the truth. Few people had survived a single night on the South Summit. She, and her *sirdar*, had been there two nights, without a tent or bivouac bag, or, we presumed, oxygen. They were dead. I felt sick.

I didn't know Mrs Pasang Lhamu but she was a national heroine, her face plastered on billboards across the country; I knew it was her fourth attempt to climb the mountain; and I knew her husband was at Camp 2, so distraught that he couldn't be persuaded to leave his tent. But I had never met her; I didn't know what she looked like, or the sound of her voice. So why was I so upset by her death? Was it compassion? Or the realization that she died where we were about to go? And that she, like me, was a woman?

I couldn't sleep that night. My head was full of horror and fear. Perhaps if she had fallen or slipped, I could have justified her death. But she hadn't. She died because she had been too high for too long – that was all. It was a turbulent night. Avalanches crashed and ice towers collapsed, who knew where, in this vast, dangerous amphitheatre. All night the glacier creaked and groaned, and with each ominous crack I felt sure the tent, with me in it, would be swallowed into the ground. Another crash! I sat bolt upright, quaking. Outside I could see a light. The Sherpas were preparing for a carry through the Icefall. Please God, let them be safe. Please, no more deaths – not our friends. Every crash, I was sure, must be across their path. Please, not Ang Passang, not Kami Tchering.

The following morning, I don't think I've ever been so pleased to see anybody as I was these two Sherpas, bathing in the sunshine with their friends.

'How's your finger?' asked Ang Passang.

'Fine, fine,' I said, hopping across the rocks to show him. 'Just pleased you're fine.' He looked perplexed.

I strolled back to my tent to catch up on sleep, getting up only for lunch. Mrs Pasang Lhamu's death was still troubling me. 'Hey,' said John, 'don't let this upset you, we'll look after you.'

For a good couple of weeks now we had been mulling over those words of advice offered by Chris Bonington at Gorak Shep. Before he made a final push for the summit, he had taken a break from the mountain and strolled down the valley, through Gorak Shep, through Lobuje, and on to the village of Pheriche, at around 14,000 feet, for a couple of days. Here, where the air is thick, he recharged his batteries for what turned out to be a successful bid for the summit. We had since learnt that a New Zealand commercial team on the mountain with us had employed the same tactics the year before, which, perhaps, had had something to do with their unparalleled success. All but one of their clients had stood on the top.

'Let's do it,' cried Andy, suddenly decisive. 'Let's pack our bags and go. Two o'clock?' And that was it. With no further debate, he and Peter were committed.

But not me. I wanted very much to go and had been toying with the idea with John for a while. I had assumed that at some stage we would take a break, and now, when the opportunity was upon us, John's enthusiasm waned, not just for himself, but for me too. Perhaps it was down to noble idealism, in which John excels, that a team should be as a single entity so that if a few of us went, we all should. But as I pointed out, not all of us *could* go. The 'B' team as John dubbed them – 'B' for Best, Bill and Harry and Dave Walsh – had plans to move back up the hill the next day. Indeed, not everyone wanted to go. At two o'clock I watched Andy and Peter stroll off down the glacier towards Gorak Shep, wondering how they had succeeded in ignoring John's will.

John came round, of course, when it had started to snow and it was too late for me to go. By the next morning, he had decided to stay, as leader, but wished me well. 'Enjoy yourself,' he said. 'Stay a couple of nights, there's plenty of time.' I set off alone. In my sack I carried a tent, a sleeping bag, karrimat, duvet jacket, head-torch, water-bottle, a bar of chocolate, and a book, and strolled down the icy glacier on holiday, as free as the air.

I thought that I might perhaps stroll the four or five hours to Lobuje that day, but even before I had reached the tiny hamlet of Gorak Shep it was snowing. I stopped at a teahouse for a mug of chocolate. It was deliciously warm and womb-like inside, and before my eyes had grown accustomed to the gloom, a young man leapt to his feet and grabbed my hand. 'You must be Rebecca!' he said. 'I'm Mel and this is my girlfriend Tina.' (Clearly, Andy and Peter had been doing the rounds.) There was a Swedish journalist too, kitted, most oddly, in safari gear, and an Israeli couple still recovering from an eighteen-month tramp around the dusty streets of India. The six of us sat huddled on a wooden bench in this dark, smoky little dwelling, and whiled away the afternoon, chatting, eating, and drinking one round of hot chocolate after another. The proprietors insisted we wrote down each order we made in big bold letters in a little notebook. 'HOT CHOCOLATE 8 rupees', or 'OMELETTE, TWO EGGS 45 rupees'. Perhaps they couldn't understand our accents or maybe we were inadvertently doing their accounts for them. Rumour had it that the young Tibetan refugee couple who ran this teahouse had had to find the equivalent of £1,000 for the required permit. A family could live several lifetimes in the Khumbu on £1,000! The story went that the couple had succeeded in borrowing the money off a wealthy wretch in Namche who charged them interest at 50 per cent, and each month the husband would walk to town and apologize for not repaying his debt in full.

Here, though, in their home (for at night, when we tourists retired to a little bunkhouse out at the back, or else to a tent, pitched in the wilderness outside, they would lie down to sleep on the wooden benches where we were sitting), they looked content enough, she particularly, her face glowing in motherhood. Parcelled in blankets in a small wooden box in the corner of the room was a baby, its little brown face gleaming like a polished hazelnut. She was perfect, smiling on demand, and clamping inquisitive fingers with tiny hands, like a vice. Every so often her mother would pick the little bundle up and pass her lovingly from one admiring guest to another, or else, gathering a long length of cloth, strap the baby to her back, where, in silence, the little one watched, with giant brown eyes, over her mother's shoulder as she peeled the skins of newly boiled potatoes for our supper. Occasionally, as the afternoon passed, I'd wander to the door to check the weather, my conscience nagging. The purpose of this adventure, after all, was to walk down to Lobuje, or even Pheriche so that I could regain a little strength. But it continued to snow. When at last a flat calm fell on the darkening landscape and the snow had stopped, I picked up my rucksack and slithered down a little hill into a broad and perfectly flat-bottomed valley surrounded with fluted hills, like a large, oval flan dish. Here, I decided, I would spend the night.

I felt a little vulnerable, alone in the fading light, scouring this snowy desert for rocks to pin down the guy-ropes of my tent, but once they were secured, and I was safely inside, I consoled myself with a 'You're fine, Rebecca,' and 'There's no danger here', spoken aloud, just to make sure I would listen, and snuggled into my sleeping bag with a book.

The next I knew the light and warmth of morning sunshine was radiating through the canvas of my tent. I rolled over and stuck my head out of the door to see the most glorious of blue skies. It was hot, like a late spring day on the ski slopes, the snow squidgy and wet, melting around the tent. I strolled up to the teahouse and ordered an omelette, two eggs, please, with cheese, and three mugs of chocolate, and lay stretched out on my back on a bench in the sunshine, soaking up the sunshine like a lizard. I have no idea how long I lay there – an hour, perhaps, maybe two. It must have been lunchtime, at a guess, when flopping my head to one side I spotted Andy and Peter striding purposefully down the hill towards me, from the direction of Lobuje. 'It's been a cocktail party!' said Peter.

'I know,' I replied, rolling to my feet, 'I met half the guests.'

'Pheriche to here in three hours. Not bad, eh?' he enthused. Not bad at all. Clearly the Bonington-style breakaway had done him good. Such were his exuberance, verve and gusto, not to mention his intention seemingly to break all land speed records between Pheriche and here and, presumably, here and Base Camp, that I wondered if he'd resent being offered a cup of tea.

'A drink?' I proposed, tentatively.

'Well, all right,' he replied, with much watch-checking and whirring of brain. Perhaps they'll mentally lop off a tea-break from their overall time, I mused.

We were joined by two Sherpas, Lopsang and Tashi. They

were the nephew and grandson respectively of the most celebrated Sherpa of all, Tenzing Norgay. It seemed odd, and somehow a privilege, forty years on from Tenzing's historic ascent of Everest, to be sitting with his descendants, drinking tea. 'You know,' said Tashi, excitedly, 'I've just had a letter from Buckingham Palace. The Queen has invited me to a fortieth anniversary celebratory lunch!'

His uncle Lopsang was quieter, and didn't look like a Sherpa, I thought. I would have supposed he was Korean. He and Tashi were heading, like me, for Lobuje. 'We'll walk together,' suggested Lopsang.

We trotted along a narrow path across a dull stretch of moraine and on, down a steep hill, skipping between the rocks, onto terra firma – and how lovely it felt to be walking on soft soil again – and on, along the valley floor, towards Lobuje. Lopsang was a most interesting man. He lived, he said, as Tenzing had, in Darjeeling and was an Indian national. Tashi, he said, was Australian, having married an Ozzie girl, and was leading an Australian 40th Anniversary Everest expedition. Lopsang was there to offer a helping hand.

It was fascinating to see how the success of one tenacious Sherpa, whose story we all knew so well, had resulted in success, not only for himself but for Lopsang's and Tashi's generations. Lopsang had been in the British army – his English was flawless. Now, following in Tenzing's footsteps, he was the chief instructor at the Himalayan Institute of Mountaineering in Darjeeling, founded after the first ascent of Everest to develop a love and knowledge of mountains among Indians. He had even visited Plas y Brenin, the mountaineering school in Wales. Lopsang's family were a cosmopolitan bunch – him in Britain, Tashi in Australia. Tashi's sister, he told me, had been a high flyer with Lipton's, in London, and now lived with her family in Delhi.

That evening, in Lobuje, the three of us sat on a rickety old wooden bench in a delightful but primitive smoky dwelling, more resembling a barn than a home, peeling 'Sherpa potatoes', as Tashi called them, dunking each one, steaming, into a little pot of salt and a deliciously spiced chilli mix. There was no running water, no electricity, no chimney – of course – and the only light was the warm glow of the wood-burning stove. Tashi, all smiles and charm in his dapper red suit, looked for all the world as if he had just walked off the ski slopes of Gstaad.

'I like your watch,' I said.

'Thank you, it's an Oyster Explorer II Rolex.'

'I know,' I said, 'I've got one.' Rolex was an obvious target for sponsorship. The company had sponsored Hunt's 1953 Everest team and several expeditions since: Reinhold Messner had a Rolex, as did Stephen Venables and Ranulph Fiennes. I had sneaked away from the office one morning to be presented with my Oyster Explorer II in a most civilized tea-sipping ceremony at Rolex's illustrious offices in London's West End, and walked away feeling as if I had just been inaugurated into a rather special, élite Rolex explorers' club. What I was about to learn was that Rolex had given Tashi's expedition not only a watch but also $10,000. There was more to come. It turned out that Lipton Tea, not Rolex, was Tashi's main sponsor. (We had, by chance, approached Typhoo Tea, and got nothing.) 'And Thai Airways?' I asked, pointing to the airline's logo stitched to his lapel. 'Ah, yes,' he said, 'they gave us seven complimentary tickets.' Thai had given us one complimentary ticket if we bought fourteen. 'It must be your name,' I said, to which he nodded.

I pitched my tent that evening on scrubby, flattish ground, yaks grazing all around it, amid the three or four little teahouses that comprised Lobuje, and retired to bed in an agreeable, dozy haze. I slept a full ten hours and awoke to see the amphitheatre of snowy peaks surrounding me turned a golden pink by the rising sun.

It took only a few hours to walk back up the length of the valley, through Gorak Shep, and on to Base Camp. I was feeling strong, as Peter and Andy had before me, and plonked myself in the mess tent for a hearty lunch. 'So,' I asked, tucking into a fresh supply of runny cheese, 'what's the news?'

As had been planned, the 'B' team – Bill, Harry and Walshy – had moved back on to the hill and were happily ensconced at Camp 2. The only concern seemed to be Dave Halton. He had positioned himself alongside the 'B' boys, at Camp 2, and seemed undecided whether his intent was to succumb to the boost of bottled oxygen or not, and whether indeed he would continue climbing with the 'B' team, none of whom were using oxygen, or else hang back and climb with the rest of us 'yobs', as John so aptly called us, who were. The oxygen was not yet in place at either Camp 3, on the Lhotse Face, or at Camp 4, on the South Col, where we intended to use it, so there was little point in our moving up the hill. We had, to my delight, another rest day here at Base Camp.

I decided to allocate it for washing. Once I was on the hill I knew I would wash neither hair, nor body, nor even step out of the clothes in which I stood. And so as a final luxury, I asked the cook boy, tentatively, if he might spare me just one little bowl full of water. Water was a precious commodity, carried from a stream a hundred yards or so from camp. He smiled and generously ladled some cold into a bowl and added a mug or two of hot to take off the chill, then handed it to me. With this cumbersome load, I tottered gingerly, from rock to rock, to my tent. It's quite extraordinary the pleasure that can be taken from an activity that at home might be considered so basic. For a happy hour I scrubbed my hair, and then my body, in the same soapy water, and then my socks, laying them in a little line on a rock to dry. It was a warm, glorious day at Base Camp, one for sunbathing and burying my head in a book; though for those at Camp 2, we learnt, over supper, the day had been a very different one.

Sitting in our down suits, with bowls of soup in the mess tent, all of us – Peter and Jan, the two doctors and the Base Camp team, Sandy Simpson and Noel, Wyn and Brian, and me – listened, as if in some important board meeting, to what our chairman had to say. John said, somewhat glumly, that he had just had a lengthy chat with the boys at Camp 2, over the radio. The news was thus: Bill, Harry and Walshy had found themselves ahead of the other expeditions on the mountain and were anxious to make a bid for the summit. There was no problem here, as far as we could see. Dave Halton, he said, after long and painful hours of deliberation had decided he would join them, which again, none of us could see as a problem. The concern, as John explained it, was that the snow, high on the hill above the South Col, lay particularly deep and might prove prohibitively cloggy for them to wade through. Now, *this* I understood. In 1989 not one of the climbers in Tibet had succeeded in climbing Everest for this reason. But here came the crux: the 'B' team had made a request for John to send up some of the Sherpas – who might otherwise have accompanied us – to blaze a trail for them.

'Huh!' I cried. 'What about Bill's bloody ethics?' Hadn't it been Bill who declared unabashedly that climbing Everest with oxygen was like taking a stroll along Brighton beach? And now he wanted Sherpas! And Sherpas, what's more, who would be using oxygen.

There was more. One of the 'B' team had apparently made it perfectly clear that not one of us yobs (with the exception of John, and John, being John, would stick with us) had a chance in hell of making it beyond the South Col, so what did it matter if we had fewer Sherpas? The atmosphere was palpable, nerves were frayed and egos bruised. 'Absolutely no compromise should be made,' was the cry.

'Now come on, they're only asking for a helping hand,' John reminded us. 'We want *someone* on the top.'

I couldn't say what was on the minds of any of my team mates that night, as each one, a little shocked, or disappointed, perhaps, tottered off into the night to his tent, and sleep. But in my mind things were quite clear. They could have all the Sherpas and whatever oxygen they needed, but please *not* Ang Passang and Kami Tchering.

It was with relief, then, that after a night's sleep and a few hours to calm our nerves, we all calmly agreed on this compromise. 'Let them have two of the Sherpas, or three if they so wish but not Ang Passang and Kami Tchering,' was the consensus. Those at Camp 2 agreed – and even apologized for their impertinence.

It took a couple of days to position the Sherpas and the

oxygen on the South Col so we were delayed. We relaxed. 'What,' said Peter, earnestly, 'if we bagged the summit and were home in time for the dinner?' His wife, Emma, was to host a fund-raising dinner in aid of the Himalayan Trust at the Carlton Tower Hotel on 11 May. 'But Peter, tomorrow's May the first.' How on earth he imagined we could climb Everest and be home in under a fortnight, I didn't know – there was no limit to his optimism. 'Well,' he went on, 'we'll be on the top on the eighth, back here on the ninth, helicopter to Kathmandu on the tenth, and charter a plane.'

'A Lear jet, maybe?'

'And then, I suppose,' said some smart-arse, 'we could abseil off the chandeliers in our wind-suits?'

Chapter Eight

———•·•———

IT WAS A Sunday, 2 May, and the day of reckoning. We were to pack our sacks, don harness, boots, crampons and our warmest clothes and leave the security of Base Camp for the penultimate time. We had had our practice runs. This third and final time we were climbing through the Icefall and along the length of the Western Cwm, on to the South Col, and thence to the summit. Next time we left Base Camp would be for home.

One by one, we gathered in the mess tent, helped ourselves to mugs of milk or tea, from one of the now familiar Chinese flasks. It was 3 a.m., earlier than any of us might have liked. Today the plan was to climb to Camp 1 and along the length of the Western Cwm to Camp 2, with luck, before the Cwm turned into a raging furnace in the midday sun. 'I've been thinking,' said Peter, 'is it worth my while going up the hill, eating all that food at Camp 1 and Camp 2, only to be sick?' And in unison, we yelled, '*Yes, it bloody well is!* Peter, you're coming!' It was preposterous to think that the man whose brain-child the Everest expedition had been, and who was responsible for each of us being on it, shouldn't go with us. It took a while to persuade him, but finally he relented. As we watched him stumbling into the darkness to collect his kit, Sandy whispered, 'Peter never could make decisions in the morning, you know,' and, 'he needs a little help.'

We all needed help, of course. I often wondered if I could have made it through the Icefall without the companionship of those around me. We stood, the five of us – John, Sandy, Andy, Peter and me – outside the tent in the dark, pulling on gloves, hats and rucksacks, preparing to move off. Are they frightened? I wondered. Might there be just a flicker of fear deep somewhere in John's stomach beneath that able exterior? No one spoke. No one voiced fear. I thought back, momentarily, to an evacuation at King's Cross. Shortly after the fire in 1987 I had been in the Underground when there was a bomb scare. A thousand commuters, each, surely, with the horror of those news flashes in their head, walked sedately off the train, along the platform, and up the escalators into the street, as if it was any other uneventful Thursday afternoon after a day in the office. I walked, too, as composed as everyone else. But my heart was pounding.

It pounded again, as, for the third time, we walked clumsily in our heavy boots along the rocky path meandering alongside the encampment, to the foot of the Khumbu Icefall. Crampons on, and once more we stepped in line into it. True to form, just to keep us on our toes, the Icefall had changed again since the last time we had worked our way through its corridors and cavities. Another vast cathedral of ice had come crashing down leaving the sky empty where before we had gazed up at it. Our last path was obliterated. I don't suppose anyone had walked over these ruins before us; no footsteps lay among the rubble, and ladders, once neatly horizontal, lay awkwardly, sticking out of the ice like fractured bones. It must have fallen just that night, I thought, as I picked my way across the splinters, following John and Andy. Larger chunks of ice rocked underfoot, throwing a less than sturdy body off balance. We were lost; I was convinced of it. I felt my pulse race and a tidal wave of adrenalin flood through my arms and legs, which was just as well, because ahead, Andy was embarking on a steep and seemingly never-ending icy stairway. I followed, the ice, like scree, slipping underfoot, two steps forward, one back. I aged a year in the half-hour we spent lost in the Icefall – and lost another stone in weight.

We made it. Another hour and we stood puffing at the top of the long banana-shaped ladder that marked the end of the Khumbu Icefall and the beginning of the Western Cwm – and safety. The going was easy from here. We could relax as we walked across the snow carpet that lay evenly over the gently undulating valley floor. A well-trodden path zig-zagged round either end of bottomless crevasses that cut across the valley floor. Over one more knoll and there at last we saw the gathering of tents that was Camp 1.

It was still in a cool morning shadow when we arrived, and for an hour or so the five of us sat in a tent in a knotted heap, five pairs of arms, legs and cumbersome boots entwined like a modernistic statue, sipping tepid orange juice from a billy, until the sun rose over the ridge and it was suddenly warm. I don't know why we moved on, along the Western Cwm to Camp 2 in the heat of the day. 'Why not rest here and leave in the morning, before sunrise?' I asked John, to which he answered, 'To see if we can do it.'

The path, familiar now, which swept either end of the vast crevasses, was almost level, easy on the lungs and the legs, and the temperature was tolerable for a while. For the first time since stepping on Everest, I was positioned at the front of the line, the others behind me. It was a good move: it meant that I could control the pace, not too slow, and more to the point, not too fast. It always felt, when we were walking along, as if we were tethered together by an invisible rope: if you were at the back, you were dragged along by those ahead and vice versa. I paced myself, counting footsteps all the time, not allowing myself a rest until I had reached a hundred. Then I would stop, turn to the others and ask, 'All all right?' as if it was them not me who needed a break, and trudge on again . . .

Before long the sun was high in the sky. The air was still and the Western Cwm that I had once thought beautiful was now a torturous white-hot furnace. We couldn't escape, and could hardly move. I counted thirty steps and stopped. No one argued. Everyone dropped their sacks and sat in a silent, dishevelled heap in the snow. I laid my head on my sack, and slept.

I'm told it took us six hours – I reckon it was nearer a hundred – to drag ourselves the two miles along the Western Cwm, in temperatures soaring to 130 degrees. We stepped, finally, onto the strip of moraine tucked under the West Ridge of Everest, Lhotse rising above our heads, and there, basking in the sunshine, were Bill, Harry, Walshy and Dave Halton. I could hardly summon the energy to say hello, before I collapsed, harness, boots and all, into a tent. I lay there, lumps and bumps digging into me, in a doze. The next I knew it was morning.

None of us had any idea, of course, that first day in the Western Cwm, but this camp was to be home for a good few days, even weeks. It was home for far longer than any of us would have chosen, much too long for our boredom thresholds and health: the camp was at over 22,000 feet, and the oxygen level was well under half of what it would have been at sea level.

Andy, our resident respiratory specialist, conducted an experiment one afternoon, just for fun. It wasn't a new one. On the walk in, at Junbesi, Chukhung, on Island Peak and at Gorak Shep, and at Base Camp, he had pleaded with us, repeatedly, to place a warm finger in a little digital contraption called an oxymeter, which, miraculously, measured the oxygen level in one's blood. I hated doing this, even developed a phobia about it, because every time Andy persuaded me (against my better judgement) to do it, I was confronted with a row of flashing red numbers telling me just what I didn't want to know, which was that the oxygen level in my blood was very low – much lower than anyone else's. 'Andy, does this mean I'm not acclimatizing well?' I'd asked, thinking, 'Does it mean I'm going to peg out up there?' And he'd answer, 'No, no,' unconvincingly. 'Look, it's searching,' he would enthuse, as the figure shot up a point or two before plummeting again. 'It doesn't mean a thing.'

I wasn't reassured. Andy had told me that a healthy young person at a sensible altitude – sea level, say – has an oxygen saturation level of 97 or 98 per cent. If it dropped below 90 per cent they would be whisked immediately into hospital and given oxygen. That afternoon, my oxygen saturation level was 68 per cent.

'Why am I 68 per cent when John's 78?' I demanded, to be answered with the usual 'Doesn't matter', leaving me wondering why the hell he had bothered to take the measurement in the first place.

He conducted another experiment that afternoon, though, which he hadn't performed before. The apparatus comprised a bottle of oxygen, a regulator, a mask, the oxymeter and four victims – John, Sandy, me, and Andy himself – the aim being to record our oxygen levels when we were given various rates of supplementary oxygen, starting with one litre, then two, then three litres per minute. We took it in turns to sit on a rock, oxygen mask plugged on face and little finger in the oxymeter, while one upped the oxygen flow rates and another studiously recorded the figures. For the first time my results were satisfactory. I was thrilled that on three litres per minute I scored an oxygen level of 97 per cent! As did Andy, Sandy and John.

However, during the long, tedious days that followed on that strip of moraine in the Western Cwm, we were not on supplementary oxygen. Each day our condition deteriorated a little, we became thinner, weaker, and our minds were fuzzier, as day after day, we grew impatient.

On our first day at the camp, still weary from the 5,000-foot ascent from Base Camp, we watched our 'B' team prepare for their first ascent to Camp 3 from where they meant to climb onto the South Col, and weather permitting, to the summit. The four of them, dressed alike in fur-trimmed scarlet wind-suits, vast boots, packs loaded on their backs, stood in a semi-circle for the photograph. I thought they looked wonderful. 'Good luck,' we said to them, 'do us well', and off they went, Harry first, then Walshy, Bill and Dave.

The rest of us stayed put. Occasionally, standing outside the cook tent, or whiling away the time on a lump of rock, we would squint up at the great slab of Lhotse that rose above us: there, on the hairline crack that was the rope were four little dots, one above the other. They seemed perfectly stationary, and only if we turned away for a while, and then turned back, could we detect their tiniest progression.

When they made it to Camp 3 (in record time, as it happened), they radioed down, as had been planned. 'Only one problem,' they said, 'there are no drinks.' But John and I, who had been at Camp 3 last, had left hundreds – sealed paper bags of chocolate, lemon juice, orange – stuffed in the pockets all around the tent.

There are advantages to there being crowds on a mountain, fixed ropes being one. However, the disadvantages include theft which leaves a nasty taste in the mouth. And the question of what to do.

Harry and Co. had fuel; they could melt snow. But it would take a monumental effort to drink enough of it to prevent them dehydrating. Perhaps Ang Passang or Kami Tchering would take some up? They agreed a price with us and set off up to Camp 3, returning in time for tea. I wondered again, as I frequently did, what on earth we would do without them.

Their effort, sadly, was in vain. As extraordinary and as bewilderingly out-of-place as it seemed, high on this snowy glacier, we were sent a daily weather forecast from the meteorological office at Bracknell. It was faxed by satellite to Base Camp, and transmitted by radio to wherever we were on the mountain. Today it was bad, and the following morning Harry, Bill, Walshy and Dave came back down the ropes to Camp 2.

I woke up that morning realizing just how goddamn uncomfortable this place was. In a perfect world I would have gone to sleep in a warm weatherproof sleeping bag, a fleece tucked under my head and the tent zipped up tight against the elements. However, I needed ventilation and the air to circulate, which meant leaving a flap open at either end of the tent with the wind whistling around the Cwm. It was a question of getting the balance right: open too little and I woke up in a snowy cavern of my own frozen smog, too much and I was blown away. I never quite got it right. I tended to close rather than open the flap, and would wake up to a thin skim of hoar frost lining the tent walls and roof. One movement, just a twitch of an elbow, and the whole lot would shower down over my sleeping bag, clothes and face, an icy, shivery snowstorm. What's more, my breath would condense in a dank sausage-shaped patch along the neck of my sleeping bag, and drip down on my face, or, worse, it would freeze into a cold, disturbing lump. My throat was sore, my nose dry and my stomach agonizingly cramped. It was hell.

The days ticked by as the wind blew and the snow lay deep on the mountain. There was no way that we could climb. We read, swapped books, scribbled diaries, sorted and re-sorted kit. Work expands to fill time available, so they say, and that's exactly what it did, if you count pottering time, sitting, wrapped in a sleeping bag at the door of a tent, or perched outside on a rock or on a squashed container barrel in the cook tent, watching the world go by. I spent hours gazing at tall Americans and petite Indian women dressed in delicate shades of pink, ambling along the moraine, or taking a foray onto the snowy glacier towards the great Lhotse Face, only to return and wait, like us, for the weather. I'd watch our Sherpas stroll nonchalantly in a gang to the neighbouring

Indian women's camp and stand, all macho, chatting. I'd watch them cook, sitting cross-legged, tossing spices into the pan, rolling *momos* and beating out chapatis, chatting, singing, learning a new song, perhaps, from some tattered old book.

For four or five days we occupied ourselves as best we could. On the morning of 6 May, the Sherpas had had enough: they packed their bags and left, down the glacier in the direction of Base Camp. 'See you soon,' I called. They would be back, as soon as the weather turned. They seemed to know instinctively that a camp at some 22,500 feet was too high to hang around in for ever. They were right. Base Camp, where the air is thicker, is where we all should have been. But the thought of going back – down the length of the Western Cwm and through that hideous Icefall, and then having to spend all those tortuous hours coming back up again – was more than any of us could bear. So we waited, and hoped that in a day or two we could move.

Others were waiting too: my American friends Keith and Yan, the Basques, Catalans, Koreans and New Zealanders. 'Well,' I'd ask, with a glance at the sky, 'what do you think?' It was all guesswork. Only the Indians had any remotely reliable advice to offer. The day the 'B' team had come down from Camp 3, they had climbed to Camp 4 on the South Col, and beyond. The wind wasn't as bad as had been forecast, they said. It was the snow that had been the problem. It had been up to their waists, they said. They weren't tall, but still, that meant it was pretty deep. Five Sherpas had blazed them a trail, but the snow had defeated them.

Slowly, an idea emerged. What, it was mooted, if all the

expeditions – Indian, American, New Zealand, Basque, Catalan and us – climbed together? What if we all combined forces and blasted a motorway of footsteps through the snow?

It made blindingly good common sense. I quite liked the idea. Safety in numbers is a fallacy, of course, on Everest, but I felt more secure, more at ease, somehow, with lots of people around. A decision was made: all of us would climb together, the day after tomorrow, 8 May, and the two components of our team – the 'Bs' and the yobs – would stick together too. One logistical problem, however, had been overlooked.

At supper, we gathered inside the cook tent, Nawang ladling soup from a huge urn. Andy looked a little concerned, I thought. He explained: if all of our team climbed on the same day there would be Sandy, John, me, Dave Halton and himself plus five Sherpas, all of whom would be climbing on bottled oxygen, ten altogether. We had only eight oxygen masks.

'Well,' said Bill, as 'B' team spokesman, 'we've been thinking.' He, Walshy, Harry and Dave Halton had decided that they wouldn't climb with the crowd after all. They would climb tomorrow and take their chances alone. Their reasoning, I think, was that they didn't want to be held up in a line of punters puffing along, one behind the other. Without oxygen, they would freeze to death in the waiting. But the rationale didn't really matter: their going ahead with Dave, on oxygen, and two Sherpas, also on oxygen, meant they should be on the summit and back down again on the Col in time to free the masks for the rest of us. I watched Andy's face dissolve into relief, and winked.

Next day we watched the 'B' team put on their scarlet windsuits, rucksacks, and boots and, for the last time, surely, head across the glacier towards the Lhotse Face. In the evening – they were ensconced at Camp 3, we were still on the dull strip of moraine at Camp 2 – the sun set in a glorious molten ball into the foot of the Western Cwm. It was still, silent, and beautiful – an evening of hope. In the morning, we would be taking one more step up the hill, towards our goal.

The path to Camp 3, zig-zagging across the Western Cwm and up the steep icy face of Lhotse, was familiar. Still, at this altitude, rising to some 24,000 feet, it took all the will I could muster to lift one foot and kick it a little higher than the last – lethargy clogged every cell of my body and I had to stop and remind myself, 'Rebecca, you're climbing Everest, remember?' and think of Hunt's words, scribbled in his book, 'Mind you make it.' *MIND YOU MAKE IT*, and still, it was a couple of thousand feet of purgatory. But because it was familiar ground – I knew the lie of the land, and the ropes – and because, perhaps, we were a little better acclimatized, the climb to Camp 3 that had previously taken eight hours took just over five, and I wasn't sick.

In front of me on what was a terrifyingly narrow ledge, an icy cliff rising above, and falling below, was the lower of our two tents spilling over the edge of the precipice like treacle off a spoon. I plonked myself in a heap in the snow, rucksack still on my back and legs sprawled inelegantly in front of me. 'Here, have a drink,' said Sandy, thrusting a mug of lemon juice into my hand. There I sat, for a full half-hour. Below us stretched the Western Cwm in all its glory. It was as I might paint in my mind's eye, and indeed, as I had dreamt when a child, the perfect hanging valley, a lovely parabola rising steeply either side, unparalleled in its scale and perfectly white. Far, far below, in the corner, at the foot of the West

Ridge and the Lhotse Face, was a line of tiny blobs on a narrow strip of moraine. It was our Camp 2 and for an instant, despite being the last of the bunch to reach this extraordinary viewpoint, I felt quietly pleased with my progress.

The doctors pulled the short straw. They sandwiched themselves as best they could into the little tent, spilling off the edge of the mountain, while John and I clambered up another 40 yards or so, to a 'second storey', where our other tent was perched on a precariously narrow ledge only fractionally wider than the first. On one side of the tent there was perhaps a spare foot of ledge, no more, before the mountain tumbled away into nothingness, and on the other side, the snow, drifted high against an icy cliff, weighed heavily on the canvas, squashing it side and back. We dived in. 'Now, the oxygen.' It was here somewhere. We knew that Sandy Simpson had arranged for the Sherpas to carry and position oxygen for us from here. There should be sufficient for a night's kip and for the climb the following day to the South Col.

I looked for it everywhere, scrambling inside the tent and out, peering under rucksacks and sleeping bags, and digging into the snow drifts, until, finally, I found the bottles buried deep in a heap of snow collected in the vestibule at the back of the tent. I lifted each one out, scraped them clear of snow and ice and laid them in a neat little stack inside the tent. Now, a brew on the boil, we could relax, but for one chore. At one o'clock I was to be interviewed by the BBC – that seemed bizarre, stuck half-way up a cliff at some 24,000 feet. We had a radio which we had borrowed from the New Zealanders for the purpose. At the same time – one o'clock on the dot – John was expecting a call from Bill, who, with Harry and the two Daves, would be on the South Col.

We sat, or lay on our sleeping bags in a tiny, squashed, somewhat uncomfortable tent, half-way up the Lhotse Face. Through the front door, its two flaps hanging like curtains on a rather unusual theatrical stage, we watched Americans, New Zealanders, Spaniards and Indian women, dressed in pink, inch their way up the fixed rope to their tents, pitched another storey or two above ours. The United Nations were on the move on a glorious and sunny day.

With no warning the weather changed. The sky was blue one moment and grey the next; there was no wind and then, with a whoosh, eddies of snow swept across the Lhotse Face and into our tent. Reaching to zip up the door I saw a disgruntled figure slumped in the snow, immediately outside our tent. 'I can't go on!' he wailed in distinctly Antipodean tones. We hailed him to our tent and bade farewell to our restful afternoon. The New Zealander got his bottom inside the tent, leaving his legs and his cramponed boots outside in the snow. We zipped the door shut round his thighs, snow blowing everywhere, brushed the snow off his back, wriggled his arms into a jacket, gave him a drink, and called Rob Hall, his guide, who we presumed must be in a tent a couple of storeys up. 'We've got one of your punters,' said John, 'what do you want us to do with him?' And in half an hour we heard a rustling noise outside, unzipped the tent, gave the New Zealander an almighty heave and he was gone, just as the BBC called from London. 'And now,' we heard a distant, crackling English voice, 'we are going to make broadcasting history, live from Everest . . .' I can't remember what the questions were, but, to my relief, there wasn't one about the rubbish on the mountain, or about my being a woman. This episode over, we lounged back on our sleeping bags and waited for Bill to call, and the afternoon to pass.

But Bill never did call. An hour passed and then another. We must have fallen into a doze, when, 'John!' we heard. John leapt to the door, tearing open the zip: 'Yes, mate, what is it?'

Outside stood Dave Walsh, shivering in a whirl of snow. He crouched down and crawled inside. 'What happened, mate?' They'd been caught in the storm. 'Where?' He didn't know; an hour, or maybe two hours from the South Col. This was the problem: they didn't know where they were or how long they would have to battle through the storm to the tent pitched on the Col so they had turned back. Then Bill stumbled in, followed by Dave Halton and yet another swirl of snow.

'And Harry?' He had gone ahead, swift as ever, keeping pace with the Sherpas. With luck they'd be tucked up cosily in their sleeping bags on the South Col, though we had no way of knowing for sure. Bill was carrying the only radio.

It was distressing to see the three grey in the face, dejected and cold. Only yesterday Walshy had been steaming along like an express train. Dave was wiry and fit; and Bill, wheeze as he might, was as tough as an old boot – an Everest veteran. Now Walshy was talking of calling it a day, and Dave, sitting quietly in the corner, coughed. It was terrible.

Perhaps if there had been room they might have camped with us and given it another shot, but no: a quick warm-up, a drink, and they were off, down to Camp 2 in the sheltered corner of the Western Cwm. I felt disheartened: all optimism and confidence swept away in a flurry. There was so much snow in the tent that, with a paper tissue, I started collecting it all and pushed it into a little heap in a corner. John looked glum. I had an idea. 'Let's get the doctors round for supper.'

A passing visitor, sticking a nose in our tent and seeing the four of us huddled miserably in a heap, might understandably have thought that tragedy had befallen us. We uttered barely a word. I was cook, obliged repeatedly to reach across Andy who sat plumb in the middle of the doorway, through which, with an awkward stretch and a flick of a wretchedly weak wrist, I had to shovel dollops of snow for the pot. I nearly gave up – and finally wished that I had. The boil-in-the-bag casserole was inedible.

In the big outdoors, it carried on snowing. John radioed the New Zealanders up the hill. 'We'll talk in the morning at five,' they said, 'and make a decision then.' On which note the doctors heaved on their boots, and left.

'Are you sleeping on oxygen, John?' I asked, ferreting in my sack for my oxygen mask and regulator, to which he answered, 'No.' I unscrewed the cap of an oxygen bottle and screwed in its place a long rubber tube connecting the bottle to the regulator and the mask. I put a fetching orange skull cap with a little strip of black Velcro over each ear, to which I stuck the two corresponding strips of Velcro on either side of the mask. I snuggled into my sleeping bag, turned the dial to half a litre per minute, stuck a woolly hat over my skull cap, plugs in my ears, a mask over my eyes, and slept.

Chapter Nine

———•◦•———

A T FIVE O'CLOCK next morning an arm emerged
from John's sleeping bag. He picked up the radio,
called the Kiwis as planned, and with an almighty
grunt, hauled himself into action: 'We're off!' he boomed.

'Up or down?' came a cry from below. It was Sandy.

'Up!'

'Shit.'

I had slept a delicious eight hours on oxygen. The sky had
cleared and with it, so it seemed, the misery that prevailed the
previous afternoon. John radioed Bill at Camp 2, asking him
if he could instruct Ang Passang and Kami Tchering to put
on their boots and hoof it up the hill. They would pick up
our sleeping bags on the way and meet us on the Col. No
problem. Then John briefed the boys at Base Camp. 'We're
packing up and giving it a go,' he said, 'just as soon as we're
ready,' which, he pointed out, might be a little while. What
with the BBC thing, and the Kiwi collapsing in our tent, and
then our three guys dropping in for a little sustenance, we had
had little time to do that all important thing: drink. We
shovelled and melted snow, and drank mug after mug of
whatever powdered drink we could find stuffed in the pockets

of the tent – anything, so long as we could get it down. Come eight o'clock, and I had only one thing left to do. Peter was on the radio from Base Camp. 'Becks, can I ask a big favour? Various TV stations would like a quick thirty seconds from you, just a kind of wrap-up of what the plan is for today, and then later in the day it will be broadcast. Do you mind doing that? Over.'

'When are you talking about, Peter? Over.'

'Now. Just a thirty-second soliloquy as they call it. Over.'

'OK, Peter. Would you like me to include about the "B" team or just stick to our own programme here? Over.'

'I think just stick to your own programme. Over.'

'OK, I'll do that when you're ready. Over.'

'We're ready now. Your sound level is looking pretty good, according to Noel, who isn't looking so good' – peals of laughter rumbled into the tent from Base Camp – 'he's got a hangover. So, Becks, when you're ready.' And so I gibbered on for thirty seconds, about oxygen, and having had a good night's sleep, about feeling chirpy and optimistic. 'Becks, that was perfect, very good indeed. Over,' crackled Peter.

'Hey,' I cried, 'Sandy's on the rope already. I'd better move!'

Outside, Sandy – with no oxygen – had clipped onto the fixed rope, and joining the Americans, Indians, and Spanish, was making his way up the hill. Now, my rucksack. I squeezed out of the tent and stood on the single square inch of flat ground, crampons strapped to my feet and oxygen bottle tucked in the long, cylindrical pocket stitched into the sack at my feet. The bottle should lie snugly the length of the spine with the connecting tube running out of the top of the sack and to the mask. This was fine. The problem – and a major problem at that – was the weight: the sack with oxygen was so heavy that I could hardly lift it off the ground. The oxygen bottle alone weighed a hefty 6.5 kilos, I'm told; at this altitude it felt like a lorry load. And that was without the brass attachments and regulator, plus a couple of litres of water (another 2 kilos), spare gloves and socks, a jacket, a head-torch, penknife, and a bar of chocolate. I heaved it onto a shoulder and all but collapsed. I wondered if the oxygen was worth it? Sandy clearly thought not. And for whatever reason, John, too, had opted not to carry oxygen. Only Andy, as respiratory specialist, and I had burdened ourselves with these onerous tanks. I watched Andy stumble the few feet to the fixed rope. I twiddled my regulator to 2 litres per minute, struggled across and clipped in behind him. Behind me was John.

I knew then how a cart-horse must feel when it is first harnessed in all that leather and blinkers. The load knocked my balance haywire; and the mask and the goggles, crowding my face, were distressingly claustrophobic. The goggles steamed up, of course, restricting my vision to forward only, or down. If I wanted to see left or right I had to turn my whole body – and that mask and the bloody oxygen tank with it. Slowly and clumsily, I took a few tentative steps, the sound of each breath fighting through the mask amplified into a thunderous roar. Only once before had I been so acutely aware of my breathing and that was scuba-diving. It had been relaxing, and fun, this, I thought, was more than I could bear.

The path, like a steep, snowy staircase, led directly up the great slab of Lhotse alongside the seracs amid which the other parties had pitched their tents. There were, perhaps, sixty of us on the rope, maybe more; but for those first few steps, ungainly and painfully slow, I was conscious of the one, right behind me. 'Fucking chance you've got of climbing Everest,' he said scornfully. I fought not to dwell on that and concentrated on putting one boot in front of the other. Slowly, as I grew accustomed to the load and accepted the claustrophobia, the going became a little easier.

I was glad of the crowd on the rope. They set the pace – a slow one, I'm happy to say. Only a superman – Harry, perhaps – could have found the strength to abandon the rope, kick fresh tracks in the snow and accelerate past a climber in front. I relaxed, found a rhythm, and as an unknown figure ahead of me inched a little higher, a little closer to the Col, I filled his steps, maybe five or six paces behind him.

At a point where the ropes no longer led straight up a 'stairway' but turned sharp left, traversing the Lhotse Face, I unclipped from the rope and, with John, stepped to one side and kicked a deep bucket seat in the snow. Perched high in this eagle's nest, for the first time that day we were able to study the glorious view. It was my vision of my perfect valley, and, if we glanced over our shoulders, we could see across the expansive Lhotse Face, a line of people marking the path we had yet to manoeuvre, across the snowy slopes to a rocky protrusion called the Yellow Band, and on again, in a broad parabolic sweep, like a skipping rope, to the crest of the Geneva Spur. Beyond this, hidden from view, was the South Col.

We rested a good while here, drinking, chatting, chewing on a bar of chocolate – quite relaxed – waving and nodding at passers-by. 'Hi, Lopsang!' He joined us, with Tashi. 'John, have you met? Lopsang was at Plas y Brenin, in 1986.' It was really most agreeable and convivial – comfortable, even – provided you didn't have to move.

Which, of course, we did. A few hundred yards ahead, I spotted Sandy in the crowd – red suit, pale blue rucksack – almost at the Yellow Band. The path we followed to this point was just a stroll, really – horizontal, almost – but among the rocks, I gasped what I thought to be my last breath. This was John's territory. He leapt ahead, leaving me floundering, kicking my crampons into an unforgiving lump of rock. I was stuck. I looked up. There, just a few yards above, was Lopsang, flask in hand, calmly offering me a drink. 'Some tea?' he said, all concern. I hate tea! 'Thank you, Lopsang,' I muttered into my mask, and with a final, panic-stricken tug on the rope, scaled the rock with a series of quick little kicks and collapsed, gasping, at his feet.

'Tea?'

The ground was level here. A few more paces and then I planted myself in the snow, and downed what was left of my orange juice. I didn't drink much as a rule – a day in the hills and my climbing chums are gasping for a pint while I'm left wondering what all the fuss is about. Drink, as distinct from booze, I can take or leave – except on a mountain. Without a drink on Everest I was as a stove without gas. I couldn't operate.

I continued along the path with John. Again it was a stroll, really, across a slope we might have skipped along in twenty minutes in the Alps. Here it took the best part of a couple of hours, eyes glued to our feet, pack heavy, pacing five, maybe six paces in succession, then resting, catching the air, and moving slowly on. A little way across, looking up, I saw two scarlet figures coming down from the Geneva Spur. It was Tcheri Zhambu and a friend who the day before had raced the storm to the Col with Harry. In minutes, they were unscrewing water bottles, offering us a drink. 'Harry? Oh, he's fine,' they said. 'Why are you coming down?' I asked, to which they answered, quite matter-of-factly, that there weren't enough oxygen masks for everybody. They were wonderful. They went on down with seemingly not a care in the world, leaving John and me to plod a little higher towards the summit.

As I trudged up the final sweep of the rope, I twiddled my regulator to three litres of oxygen per minute. It was steep, the snow was deep, and, looking up, all I could see was the crest of the Geneva Spur, brilliant white, gleaming against a gorgeous blue sky. A few more steps and we would be over that crest, and then, surely, only minutes from the South Col.

What a view! Just over the lip of the crest, I sat down in the snow with John and Andy; perched just above us were Lopsang and Tashi – and felt intense pleasure in just being alive. Stretched below us was what must surely be one of the greatest wonders of the world, the Western Cwm. As I looked down from a bird's eye view upon this secret valley, it was almost like sitting on the wing of an aeroplane: five thousand feet below, I could see the track we followed, a thin pencil line, snaking along the length of the valley floor from the head of the Khumbu Icefall. Beyond was Pumori, a 7,000-metre monster reduced to ice-cream cone proportions; and beyond that, peeping through the cloud, one of the great 8,000-metre peaks, Cho Oyu, in Tibet. We were looking across directly on a level with its summit.

We were now at 26,000 feet; and over our shoulders the

upper reaches of Everest rose another 3,000 feet – the height of Snowdon – into the sky. Everest hides itself well, revealing itself slowly, in sections, so that it was only now that we could see what lay ahead of us. Above, reaching into the sky, was a mountain as triangular and as perfectly fashioned as a 'proper' mountain should be. It was black, covered in a sugary coating of snow; and on its face, descending into the upper slopes of the Col, we could mark our route. Leading directly up a gully in the middle of the face, to about half-way up, it veered to the right across the face to the far-right horizon, or South East Ridge. Here we would turn a sharp left and follow the length of the ridge to the pinnacle called the South Summit, the highest point on earth that we could now see. Behind this, still out of view, was the summit ridge that led to Everest's true summit, at 29,028 feet. Sitting there, relaxed in the sunshine, it all looked so easy. No problem, I thought. I was convinced we could do it.

We got up and walked around and down a little, following a line of ropes along a rocky path, to the South Col. Our first glimpse of this famous spot, written about in the journals and books of many mountaineers who had come this way before us, was extraordinary. It was late afternoon, the air was still, the sky blue, and in front of us, in this desolate spot, was a colony of some twenty or more tents – each one the latest model, compact, domed, in vibrant shades of red, yellow and silver. Between them, in little clusters, stood our climbing companions from every corner of the world, dressed in large multicoloured all-in-one suits. Some stood chatting, while others stood nonchalantly holding radios, as if conducting business on a portable phone.

On the edge of this high-altitude encampment were two muddy mustard tents, pitched by the Sherpas for us. Sitting outside one, relaxed, looking particularly dapper in his primrose yellow suit, was Harry. I ripped off my mask and dropped my monstrously heavy sack. 'What's the news?'

He had made it comfortably to the Col ahead of yesterday's storm, as we had thought, but his intention to climb on to the summit that night had been scuppered by high winds. He would be climbing tonight, with an Ozzie whose plan was also to go on without oxygen. It was difficult to imagine how Harry, having spent twenty-four hours at 26,000 feet without oxygen, succeeded in looking so fresh. With the air of a waiter at a cocktail party, he sauntered from person to person topping up mugs with orange juice, while I sat, absorbing the scene around us.

The Col was vast. I had read somewhere that it was a plateau the size of several football pitches. A hundred yards or so across this flattish, rocky ground lay a broad, glassy band of ice, above which our route led straight up the gully, and right, onto the South East Ridge to the South Summit. Behind us rose the steepening slopes of Lhotse, a mountain which, in the shadow of its famous neighbour, is the fourth highest in the world. In cross-section these two giants, the wind-swept plateau between, formed a saddle, or indeed, as its name suggests, a col. To the west it fell away slowly at first, and then abruptly into the Western Cwm. And to the east? I could see nothing – only sky. I never did go across to look over the eastern lip of the Col. No one did. Curiosity might have led us anywhere else in the world, but not here – not where taking a single step requires a monumental effort of will. I know only from books that over the eastern lip of the Col, the mountain falls away down the Kangshung Face, into Tibet.

In this wilderness, temporarily tamed by the amiable gathering in which we found ourselves, we peeled into tents, Harry, with Ang Passang and Kami Tchering, into one and John, the two doctors and myself into the other. Here, packed like sardines in a tin, we fiddled and twitched, first to establish our territory and second to rig the oxygen bottles that lay, icy to the touch, around the tent: one bottle between two when resting. Finally, the appropriate 'Y' tube attaching a single bottle to a pair of masks, we propped ourselves up, half in and half out of our sleeping bags, while John, at one end, fixed a brew. 'Well, look at you lot!' It was my American friend Keith, his piercing blue eyes peering through a little opening in the door. We must have looked a sight, like aliens, all tangled in tubing and masks. He left, and pitched a tent next to ours with Yan.

A doctor on either side of me, clamping me securely in the middle, I had it in mind that we would be making a bid for the summit in just a matter of hours, that night. This, I understood, is what people did. It was accepted practice to arrive on the Col during the day, rest for a while, and set off in the middle of that night, the thinking being that a night and another day's rest at such altitude might be detrimental rather than beneficial.

And then there was the weather forecast. Bizarre as it seemed (I never could get used to this), Bracknell had been religiously faxing reports through to Base Camp where Peter radioed them to us on the Col. At 30,000 feet, the forecast for tomorrow, relevant if we were to set out that night, was for 22-knot winds, temperature minus 32°C – not perfect, but not bad either. The following day, the forecast at the same altitude was 39-knot winds, and for the day after that, 65 knots. Clearly, the weather was deteriorating. A forecast is, of course, far from guaranteed, but if we were to use them as a guide, then – in my humble opinion – that night was the night to go.

I was soon to discover, though, that I was alone in thinking that. The doctors stated categorically that they couldn't go. 'You can go, but we're staying,' said Sandy. Andy wasn't feeling at all well. He was behaving oddly, still sitting only half in his sleeping bag, refusing to tuck himself in to keep warm; and he took an age, and only after repeated requests, to zip up the door of the tent.

John's decision was a final one and, I accept, an entirely noble one. At the time I could have cheerfully killed him. Andy was poorly, for sure; and when I think he might have been seriously ill, I feel ashamed, but in my desperation that night I just fixed in my head Sandy's words: 'We're staying, but you can go', and was mad at John for not even discussing it. 'You're exhausted', that's all he could say. 'Andy's sick and it's windy,' which it was – the wind picked up as darkness fell. 'And that,' he bellowed, 'is that!'

I felt wretched. At about eleven o'clock I heard Harry, shuffling outside the tent, preparing to give it a shot. 'John, your Sherpas want to go,' he called. I thought for just half a second that John might change his mind. But no. He grunted and rolled over to sleep.

It wasn't a restful night, as cosy as I finally found myself, snuggled up with a doctor on either side. I woke, at about half past one, to the sounds of talking, zips, and crampons scraping on rock. People, a whole crowd of them, were preparing to make a bid for the summit. I sat bolt upright. 'John,' I cried, 'we must go!'

But we didn't, of course. It would have been too late, anyhow, to rustle up drinks, sort the oxygen, and still give ourselves a fair chance of making it up and down again before nightfall next day. I miserably popped a sleeping pill, plugged my ears and lay down to concentrate hard on sleep.

When I woke again it was day and our tent once again a muddy mustard colour. The wind was still blowing and the canvas rustling. 'See,' said Sandy, 'the weather's no good for the summit.' I wasn't convinced.

Our GP's mind was made up, though, as was our respiratory physiologist's. They had called it a day. They would pack their bags and say goodbye to the South Col, and the summit, and rattle down the ropes to Camp 2. There was only one thing Andy wanted to do first, and that, with the dedication of a scientist to his research, was to take one more set of readings with his oxymeter. Each of us in turn obediently stuck a forefinger into his little machine and watched our oxygen levels flash up, while Andy, fumbling with a pencil and tattered scrap of paper, recorded the figures in wobbly little columns as best his fuddled brain would allow. I took the precaution of warming my finger first, stuffing it deep in my sleeping bag, in a cosy mitten. I wanted it to score the best result for me it could, if only to boost my withering morale. To my delight, it did. On ambient air my oxygen level was 70 per cent – not high, exactly, but higher by a couple of points than it had been almost 5,000 feet down the hill. On a couple of litres of oxygen a minute, it shot up, most encouragingly, I thought, to 86.

This little experiment over, Andy packed his machinery away, with his gloves, a water-bottle, and a hat, and painstakingly struggled into his boots. He and Sandy wriggled out of the tent, and were gone.

What a ghastly mess! With the two of them gone, all the litter – tired bits of tissue paper, frozen teabags and empty drinks packets – became depressingly apparent, like all those empty beer cans and cigarette stubs at the end of a party. It was terrible. I was feeling as gloomy as I think I've ever felt, while John sat glumly, in a pile of rubbish. Ang Passang only made it worse. 'We should have gone; all those people go!' he cried, fuelling an explosion that nearly blew our tent off the Col. I asked John, 'We will go tonight, won't we?'

'Yes, yes,' he said, 'we'll go.'

I had my worries, even so; the forecast had been for 39-knot winds, and try as I might to persuade myself otherwise, I felt weaker, physically and mentally, than I had yesterday.

In the early afternoon we made a routine radio call to Base Camp. '. . . the worse the wind conditions are going to be. Over.' It was Sandy Simpson, his voice reassuring.

'Base Camp, Camp 4, I missed the first bit of that message,' said John, 'I was changing batteries.' (Bloody things; they lasted seconds.) 'I'll ask for the weather forecast in a minute. The eleventh is the only day we're interested in. We can't stay here longer than that. At the moment there's a bit of a storm raging,' he continued. 'It's actually not very cold but there's quite a strong wind. No one seems to have come down, or at least not anyone I've seen who's gone up, but I don't know how they're faring. Over.'

Several times we peered through the tent door, training our eyes on the Face, the South East Ridge and the South

Summit for any sign of life; but as yet, 'There's no sign of Harry,' said John, 'but Harry being Harry I'm not worried about him. As soon as he appears I'll let you know.'

'This is Base Camp. I got all that, John.' Sandy again. 'The forecast for the eleventh is 240 degrees, 40 knots, minus 35 degrees centigrade. And the wind will start deteriorating after that.'

'OK, Sandy. I don't know when the eleventh starts. Is that midnight their time, or midnight our time? Over.'

'That's six a.m. on the eleventh, our time. The earlier you can go the better the weather conditions will be. Over.'

'Ah, OK. Well, by six a.m., you know, we should be well up it, and I hope 40 m.p.h. isn't too bad. What was the weather forecast for today as a matter of interest? Over.'

'22 knots. Over.'

'OK. You're on. Ang Passang reckons the guys who've gone will get up. I'm not certain, but I hope they all do.'

'Camp 4, this is Base Camp. As far as we know everybody who has left the South Col so far has summited. Over.'

'OK, Sandy. Glad to hear everyone else got up. We'll try and repeat the performance later on. Unless you've got anything else, I'm going to call out now.'

So, they'd made it. A good number of those people we had shared a camp with in a sheltered corner of the Western Cwm, and climbed with up the great bulk of the Lhotse Face, and camped with again, on this lonely, desolate Col, had reached the summit and were now on their way down, triumphant. This was crucifying.

A little later in the afternoon I took a plastic bag and a shovel and, crawling out of the tent, braved the outdoors to collect some snow to melt for brews. The light was flat, the day drawing to a close, and looking up the hill at the snowy gully leading up the face, and across, to the South East Ridge, I could see a scattering of tiny figures, black specks against the snow. A Sherpa, one of the first down, stood beside me, calmly unbuckling his harness, which fell to his feet. 'Did you make it?' I asked. 'Yes, yes, make summit,' he answered.

Slowly and wearily, I carried my load back to the tent. There was no sign of Harry yet. As dusk fell we watched figure after figure descend the gully and walk contentedly, I thought, with an air of pride, down over the icy bulbous band and into camp. We watched, and watched, and watched. Among the reds, greens and blues, once, we spotted a figure in primrose yellow. This must be Harry, we thought. But as the shape drew closer, its gait was gradually revealed, then its size, and finally, its face, it was only another stranger.

Peering through the door of the tent, we watched, brewing drinks, eating, sorting the odd bar of chocolate, gloves, head-torch, for our own bid for the summit. At eight o'clock, we crawled into our sleeping bags, just for a couple of hours, before getting up again at ten, the plan being to set out at eleven. We didn't sleep.

'Look out of the door,' said John. I unzipped the tent, pulled myself up and stared outside into nothing. It was dark, completely black but for the triangular South Summit gleaming in the sky. The trickle of climbers had stopped; and still there was no sign of Harry.

This was beginning to worry us. Harry was fast on the hill and should have been back on the Col long ago. 'He must have had an accident,' I said.

I looked again and again – until, once, I peered into the dark and saw two little lights – head-torches, for sure – one high up on the mountain, just below the South East Ridge, and a second not far from the Col. I watched; the light nearest the Col hardly seemed to have moved. 'Flash the torch,' suggested John, and so I did, six times. Harry was in the SAS. He would know this international distress signal, for sure – but there was no response. Our alarm clock screamed. It was ten o'clock. Harry had been on the hill for twenty-three hours. Wide awake, adrenalin racing through my limbs, I flashed up the stove and pulled on a boot: 'We've got to do something.' Should we go now to look for Harry – it was windy, the canvas was rattling – or wait until the morning? 'The morning,' I said, as we both knew, 'might be too late.' One boot securely laced and zipped onto my foot, I looked outside to see the light of two head-torches pan over a nearby tent. I heard voices, and then saw the two lights move in the direction of the lone head-torch, not far from the Col. 'We'll wait and see what happens, then go,' said John. There was nothing else to do. John was up and out of the tent as the lights moved back towards the camp, and as they drew closer three shadowed shapes emerged, one slumped between the other two. 'British people, British people,' I heard the cry, 'we have your friend, he is dying.'

Chapter Ten

I DON'T SUPPOSE I shall forget the night of 11 May 1993, for as long as I live. It was a night of extreme contrasts.

That night I was safe. I had rattled down the ropes from the South Col to our camp in the Western Cwm, with Ang Passang and Kami Tchering, and was snuggled cosily in my sleeping bag. John, however, was hanging on to life itself on the Col. He had tried twice the day before to help Harry to his feet and lead him down the Lhotse Face to safety. But they hadn't even made the hundred yards or so across the plateau to the fixed ropes. Harry was snow-blind, kept stumbling over his own feet and was going nowhere. They had been forced to stay another night in a storm that worsened on the inhospitable South Col, at 26,000 feet.

I can't imagine what it was like. They were alone. Everybody who had been on the Col had abandoned camp and fled.

The wind blew, the tents rattled and some were clean ripped from their anchors and blown away. John, fearful that their tent might be the next to go, made a stock-pile of gloves, hats, food and drinks and stuffed them in a sack so they would have some provisions, at least, to sit out the storm behind a boulder. He rationed his oxygen, not knowing when, or if, the storm would subside and Harry be fit to go down. That night, he had, he said, 'long conversations with his Maker'.

Quite a contrast, indeed, to a dinner that was being held at the Carlton Tower Hotel in London. Tuesday 11 May: it had been in the diary a while. Everyone, and anyone, who had any connection with the expedition was to be there: sponsors, trekkers, friends, and friends of friends of climbers, trekkers, and sponsors. The Duke of Edinburgh Award team was to be there as well as Lord Hunt – who was, of course, the founder director of the Duke of Edinburgh Award Scheme as well as leader of the first expedition to climb Everest – and the great man himself, Sir Edmund Hillary. The celebration was to raise money for Hillary's Himalayan Trust. It was hard to imagine John and Harry fighting for breath in a violent storm high up on Everest's South Col while everyone at the Carlton Tower, in their finery, no doubt, with a glass of wine or port in hand, was toasting Harry's success – and while I, at Camp 2, was asleep.

I was dead to the world that night, exhausted from our episode on the Col. I slept round the clock, and awoke, refreshed, to potter to the cook tent, with Bill, Walshy, and the two doctors, only to hear yet more devastating news. Lopsang was dead. Dead? It was spoken of quite matter-of-factly. Lopsang, Tashi's uncle, whom I had met that day at Gorak Shep and strolled with to Lobuje, whom I had chatted with in the Western Cwm, and on the Lhotse Face, who had offered me tea when I panicked in the rocky band and sat with us on that glorious snowy viewpoint atop the Geneva Spur, was dead? Yes, they said. He had fallen just above the

South Col. Poor Tashi. Lopsang was a lovely man. I didn't know him well, but I had liked to think of him as a friend. We had eaten Sherpa potatoes together, and he had shown me such kindness. 'Did he make it to the top?' I asked Tashi. 'Yes, he did,' he said. 'Six of my family have climbed Everest, but only one has been killed.' Another death: with the Nepali woman and the *sirdar*, that was three in the few short weeks we had been on the mountain.

That morning, our team's drama was almost over. At ten o'clock, John, guiding Harry on a short lead, had finally set off from the South Col, this time successfully. They had made it along the rocky path leading from the Col, the wind raging, and dropped over the Geneva Spur where, high up on the Lhotse Face, we could now see them – two tiny black blobs – slowly making their way towards Camp 3. Two Sherpas went up the hill to help, and when, at last, they were at the foot of the Lhotse Face, the boys walked across the glacier to greet them, and I followed. Harry looked all but finished. With Sandy on one arm, a Sherpa on the other, he staggered maybe twenty paces before stopping, bending double from the waist to catch breath and recover his strength, and move slowly on. But he was all right. They were both all right – they were alive and safe. And Harry was something of a hero.

Peter was on the radio from Base Camp: 'The media machine has gone mad!' he cried. Harry was the man of the minute, and my mother, what's more, had been interviewed on Breakfast Television. I couldn't believe it – Peter must have misunderstood or be pulling my leg.

What was certain was that Harry's resilience was remarkable. He had been near death, snow-blind and most probably hypothermic; he had spent four nights at 26,000 feet on

Everest's South Col, a couple of which were without oxygen, and yet, the following morning, after only one good night's sleep, he was rosy-cheeked and grinning like a cat that had got the cream. With reason – he had bagged Everest at the sixth attempt, and without oxygen. The only injury he had to show for it was minor frost-bite on a big toe and a little black blob of it on the end of his nose.

We could relax. Bill, Walshy and Andy Peacock, all of whom had stayed on this strip of moraine just to see Harry and John return safely, were free to pack their sacks and go. It was a sad moment, waving a final goodbye and seeing them trotting off down the glacier towards the Icefall. Would they stay a while at Base Camp? Would we see them again, here in Nepal? Or would they gather their belongings and go home? They had jobs to go to, and families, and there was no reason for them to stay other than a sort of loyalty, perhaps, to see the expedition through to the bitter end. Only one thing was certain: their time on this mountain was over, and shortly, Sandy's, John's and my time here would be running out as well.

It felt strangely lonely at camp that afternoon. Ang Passang and Kami Tchering had left us – only to rest for a while I hoped, before returning; Dave Halton had gone, to convalesce at Base Camp with a cough. There were only two Sherpas, Sandy, John, asleep, Harry, asleep as well, resting his toe, and me. And Nawang, of course. The two of us sat in the cook tent, he busying himself with a huge, doughy mass of flour, the size of a football, beating chapatis into shape, while I drank mug after mug of lemon juice, and scribbled copiously in my notebook. I had a lot to catch up on. The last few days had been eventful to say the least: our getting to

Camp 3, the storm, and the 'B' team turning around; the oxygen, and all the hell that went with that; the South Col; all those people getting to the top – thirty-eight people stood on the summit that day, more than on any one day in the history of mountaineering; Harry's success, and near death; my retreat with the Sherpas; John, with Harry, a third night on the Col, in that awful storm and, finally, Lopsang's death. It had been a strange few days, indeed. And now, in the quiet following the storm, it was, in a sense, stranger still.

I wondered what we were going to do now. With Harry and John safely down after their horrendous ordeal on the Col, we could pack our bags and go home – the sponsors would be happy. The judicious thing would be to strike the tents and call it a day. I should forget this bloody mountain and my fanciful, childish desire to stand on top of it, and go back down, a little sadly perhaps, and disappointed, to Base Camp, through the foothills to Jiri, and Kathmandu, and home. Deep down, however, I was determined to give it another go.

I think those who had ventured high on the hill thought me mad. No one said directly that I shouldn't go, except Sandy Scott, when I first came down from the Col, exhausted: 'Please don't go up to that horrible place again,' he had said. But, then, he's a doctor, so he would. Among the others, I just sniffed a certain reticence in the air, from their lack of words or the odd quizzical look. No one could have had any idea, though, how passionately I wanted that mountain, and no one had shared my bitter disappointment in sitting on the Col, unable to fulfil my dream.

I wasn't alone. John had suggested that he would be willing to give it another go, and Dave Halton, by all accounts fit and well once more at Base Camp, was also keen. The team down there, Peter, Sandy Simpson and Noel, were irrefutably supportive.

At supper that evening I made a tentative suggestion. The oxygen bottles we had been using were British, solid and strong to meet British standards, which was great, except that the bottles were so heavy, 6.5 kilos. The weight had half killed me. Perhaps we could buy some Russian oxygen bottles from the New Zealanders. These were titanium, small, simple to use (so they said), and most important, light. It hadn't gone unnoticed that on the Lhotse Face all those who had been using them (which, indeed, was everybody on the mountain except us) had trotted past us at a rather disconcerting speed.

To my astonishment (oxygen is expensive) the idea was readily accepted without questioning. John picked up the radio and called Base Camp. How many bottles? Nine? Yes, nine would do. That'll be no problem, sir. They would go across to the New Zealand camp and see what they could do. Nine bottles would be enough for John, me, and Dave, all to have a shot at the summit. It was 13 May. If Dave joined us tomorrow we could climb to Camp 3 the following day, the South Col the next, and to the summit the day after that, on the seventeenth. The plan was fixed.

Next morning, I was in an optimistic mood as I strolled into the cook tent, only to be told by Sandy Scott that Dave had failed the fitness test. Dave had just been on the radio. He had apparently set off early to make it through the Icefall and join us here in the Western Cwm, and had turned back. He had thought, or at least hoped, that his throat had healed and that he would be able to climb with us to the summit. But it still was giving him trouble. I felt so sorry for him. He hadn't known it at the time, but when he, with Bill and Walshy, had turned back in the storm high on the Lhotse Face, he had been, he later learnt, when talking over every agonizing step with Harry, just under the lip of the Geneva Spur, only a quarter of an hour, maybe twenty-five minutes, from the South Col and the shelter of our tent. So close.

Later in the morning, Sandy Scott walked Harry with his frost-bitten toe down the length of the Western Cwm to the Icefall, where Bill and Peter waited to accompany the invalid to Base Camp. Once again, I sat alone with Nawang in the cook tent, while he stoked the stove, prepared drinks, and I drank them as fast as he could ladle them from the urn. I was determined to get through those seven pints a day. The radio crackled. It was Sandy Simpson at Base Camp, with the latest weather forecast. 'Are you ready for this?' he asked. On 15 May, tomorrow, he said, the winds at 30,000 feet will be 25 knots. The day after, the sixteenth, 35 knots, and on 17 May, the day we had plans for the summit, the forecast was for 50-knot winds.

'Thank you, Sandy.' I wanted to dig a hole quietly and bury myself; better still, throw myself headlong down a crevasse – it would be quicker. If the news Sandy had just delivered was correct then any chance we thought we might have of climbing Everest on 17 May was scuppered. And we couldn't wait much longer than that. We had been high in the Western Cwm, or higher still, on the Col, for twelve days on the trot, almost a fortnight – a whole holiday, damn it. We were weak, and thin – my stomach was hollow, and my arms and legs rattled around in what had been skin-tight clothes. Our spirits were dampened. Soon it would be the end of the season. The monsoon was encroaching and from 20 May, the

Koreans, who had been maintaining the Khumbu Icefall all this time, replacing ropes and rickety aluminium ladders as one section of the ice collapsed after another, would cease their activities. This was the agreement. Everything, it seemed, was loaded against us.

Dragging myself to my feet, I trudged miserably across the moraine, duller and greyer than ever it had seemed before, to John's tent, to relay the news. He didn't say a word. He hardly even stirred in his sleeping bag – just grunted, and turned his back, to sleep. I felt completely alone. For a moment it felt as if the whole world – except me, that is – had stood on the summit on that night of the tenth, and now, triumphant, had skipped off home. Indeed, where once the New Zealanders, the Americans, the Australians and Koreans had pitched colourful homesteads, there was nothing – only empty grey patches of snow, rock and silence.

Had I cared to think, though, I knew there were other people on this lonely strip of moraine in the same predicament as me. A number of others – Keith and Yan, the Catalans, Basques and Indians – had missed the boat on 10 May too. We all had plans to climb to the summit on the seventeenth, and all faced the possibility of the plans being scuppered by the wind.

I took a wander down the moraine to find my American friends in conference in the Catalans' tent. 'Come in, have some tea,' they cried. I declined the latter and squeezed myself inside the tent to fill the only vacant canvas stool remaining. The tent was packed. There was a sparky Indian man (climbing with the women in pink), the Catalans, of course, and the Basques – all rugged and stubbly about the chin, and brightly dressed in layers of colourful fleece. There was a Russian too, distinguishable instantly by his aged kit. 'Well,' said Keith, 'we're off. We're bringing everything forward a day, the summit on the sixteenth and that means Camp 3 this afternoon. The Sherpas are saying the weather's good on the South Col.'

I sat there, in stunned silence. They were off! A second chance had presented itself and they were grabbing it. Enthusiasm rippled through the tent. 'Come along,' said Keith. But how could I? John was asleep; we would never make it. 'Then come on your own,' he suggested, 'we'll be around at Camp 3.'

'No,' I said, 'I can't.'

I stood up and walked out of the tent. What was I to do? Was I to sit and watch a second crowd saunter to the top of Everest? This was terrible. I had to talk to John.

He didn't say much. Perhaps there was nothing he wanted to say.

I went back to the cook tent: 'What are we going to do, Nawang?' It struck me then that Everest concertinaed a whole lifetime's emotional peaks and hollows into two short months. The peaks were lofty, like the moment we first stepped into the Western Cwm, or looked down upon this secret valley in all its glory from the Geneva Spur. The troughs were the deepest I had ever experienced. I wanted so badly to climb and yet how could I without John? My gut ached with frustration and bitter, bitter disappointment.

I wanted a voice to boom down from the sky, an independent arbitrator, a friend, *anyone* to decide for me what we should do. 'I can't help you there.' It was Sandy Simpson, his logical, reasonable self, on the radio.

He called back, a little while later. 'We've had a confab,'

he said. All the climbers at Base Camp – I imagined Bill, Walshy, Dave and Jan – had put their heads together: 'They think,' Sandy said, 'you should take your chances and go now.'

'Thank you, Sandy.' I put down the radio and walked outside to find Ang Passang, sitting cross-legged at the door of his tent, with Kami Tchering. 'Ang Passang, if I tell you the weather forecast for the sixteenth is for 35-knot winds, and for the seventeenth 50-knot winds, and that the others are climbing to Camp 3 this afternoon, and to the summit on the sixteenth, what do you think we should do?'

He leant his head towards Kami Tchering, and chatted briefly. 'Today, what day?' he asked. 'Today's the fourteenth.' Then, looking me straight in the eye, he said, a touch dictatorially as was at times his somewhat alarming manner, 'You and John go to Camp 3 tonight, South Col tomorrow, summit sixteenth.' It made sense, of course, on the probability tables. It just didn't account for one overriding fact: John was in bed.

For an hour or so, in a daze, I watched Keith and Yan prepare for what must surely be their final journey up the hill and, with a wave goodbye, stride purposefully across the glacier towards the great bulk of Lhotse that rose above us. Looking down our little strip of moraine I watched the Indians, too – tiny, feminine, all in pink – packing, unpacking and repacking their sacks, while chatting in little clusters as if preparing for a day's outing with a picnic. At last, my eyes still focused down the valley, I saw Sandy returning from the Icefall.

It seemed like an excuse for a tea-break. We sat in the cook tent, with John, stirred from deep slumber, and Nawang, busy as usual in the kitchen. The mood wasn't easy. It was odd, there being just the four of us, when only a couple of days ago the tent had been bursting at its seams, the lot of us scrapping for rocks on which to sit – odd, and decidedly cheerless. The onerous question – what are we to do? – still loomed. Half of me wanted to try to force a decision out of John, who was so exhausted that I feared an explosion. The other half was almost thinking of giving up. I didn't much want to talk about it any more.

After long, painful deliberation, John made his decision. 'Ideally, I'd wait and go on the eighteenth,' he said. We hadn't had a weather forecast for the eighteenth; it might be good, or bad. We didn't know. But then he said, with a number of ifs and buts in between – and this was final – we'll sleep tonight (for it was too late in the day to leave now), and start early in the morning, climbing all the way to the South Col in a day to make a bid for the summit on the sixteenth. We would catch up with the others and race the storm.

I wanted to be happy. He had decided this for my sake, I think, and I was grateful, and touched, but also drained. I was worried about this plan: John was still so terribly tired and, if I was honest with myself, I really didn't know if I could make it all the way from Camp 2 to the South Col in a day. I was slow by the men's standards. The last time I had climbed to Camp 3 it had taken me a little over five hours. And I had thought then I was going well. There would be a further seven, or maybe eight hours from there on to the Col. I feared it was too much for me.

With these feelings all a mix, I went outside to see a line of Indian women trot across the glacier towards the Face. It was late; perhaps only an hour off darkness. I couldn't have faced going after them now, not even if John, in some burst of boyish enthusiasm, had dragged me along by the hand, kicking and screaming.

I dived into my tent, grabbed my largest and warmest jacket and legged it back to the cook tent for supper. 'It's pizza,' said Sandy. This was a treat, indeed! I hadn't sniffed a pizza since we had eaten in a rather good restaurant in Kathmandu. 'It's because of the "waves" among the round-eyes,' Sandy said, with an odd sideways look. 'Nawang cooked it specially.'

Come the morning, we dragged ourselves out of bed at three o'clock as planned. I felt terrible. Sleep usually cures depression, I find – but not today. The four of us, John, Sandy, Nawang and I, sat, completely silent, in the cook tent, the gas lamp glowing. I tried to drink, and tried to eat. It seemed ungrateful not to, Nawang having left the warmth of his bed to fire up the stove. But hard as I tried, I couldn't. Sandy watched as I sipped feebly at my milk and pushed a spoon around in my porridge. The doubt I had felt about climbing to the South Col in a day hadn't gone away. If anything, at this early hour, it was worse, and finally, breaking the miserable silence, 'I'm not sure I can make it,' I said. It was true. John, still struggling with his porridge, spoke few words: 'I'll do what you want to do.' I sat, silent, miserable in my weakness. Well, that's it then, I suppose; we'll go back to bed. 'You can tell the Sherpas,' said John. Poor Ang Passang and Kami Tchering: 'Whenever weather good, you don't go,' Ang Passang cried, in one of his more bolshie moods. Now, in the middle of this bleak night, it must have seemed to them that once again the weather promised to be good (as good, anyhow, as we were likely to get), and once again we wouldn't go. I stumbled out into the darkness and crouched at the door of their tent. 'I'm sorry, Ang Passang. We try for the summit on the eighteenth. Maybe the weather will be good then.'

We slept, to wake up again at a respectable hour when darkness had lifted and the world looked altogether friendlier. Mid-morning, and Sandy Simpson, sound and steady as ever, was on the radio with our daily weather report, 'Want to hear the news?' The forecast for the eighteenth, at 30,000 feet' – I listened with bated breath, this was crucial – 'is for winds of 45 knots; and on the nineteenth, 30,000 feet again, winds of 50 knots.'

It was all over. Our chance was blown. A storm was moving in: 50 knots, I think Sandy had said for the seventeenth; now, 45 knots for the eighteenth, and 50 knots again on the nineteenth. It would be impossible for us to inch our way along the summit ridge in those winds – and to wait until the twentieth, maybe, or even the twenty-first, when the storm, perhaps, would have passed. Too late: the Koreans would have abandoned the Icefall. The season was drawing to its close, the monsoon encroaching – and we were all growing tired. 'Next month soon; next month summer month,' I had heard the Sherpas whisper. Their thoughts were no longer of snows, summits and skies; they had drifted, far away, to their villages and valleys, to cold beers in Namche, to holding their wives and cuddling their tiny children. And who could blame them?

There was only one thing to do: if we were to give this mountain one final shot, we must go now, this afternoon. We must be at Camp 3 tonight, to be on the South Col tomorrow, and the summit on the seventeenth. Damn the forecast! We must run, take our chances! With luck, perhaps we can beat the storm to the summit.

It is easy to theorize and plan – but how very hard to put words so easily spoken into action. Should we take this gamble and climb this afternoon, despite the forecast? Or should we not? The weather forecast for 17 May, the only day left as an option for the summit, was for 45-knot winds. I convinced myself that we would be walking into failure. We would climb to the Col only to have to retreat once more. Our chance of success, I thought, was no more than one in a hundred.

'You're a realist,' said Sandy, the doctor. 'I'd have said three to four per cent.'

He didn't want us to go. I think he thought it foolish, and he was genuinely concerned about our safety and health, as you might expect of a GP. Even the Sherpas had lost their seemingly irrepressible optimism. 'Do you think we'll make it, if we go?' I asked Ang Passang. 'Maybe,' he said, flicking his dark eyes, 'maybe not.'

John had retired to bed. I wished he hadn't. Any will that I might once have had to climb this mountain was waning fast. I was giving up. I needed an encouraging hand. If I was to continue, to find the strength to fight my way back up that hill, I needed to be persuaded and cajoled, and the only person who could do that was asleep. Back and forth I walked, from my tent to the cook tent, and from the cook tent to my tent, looking down at my feet, and up at the great bulk of Lhotse rising high above us.

Should we go? On the one hand, I argued, Sandy and the

Sherpas think our chances are slim. But on the other hand, Rebecca, there's always the possibility they are wrong. But the South Col is a frightening, dangerous place. Do you really want to put yourself through that again? But you know now how to get down: a hundred yards across the plateau and you can clip on to the fixed ropes, and you're safe, remember? But I'm so tired. Surely you can keep going for another couple of days. But the forecast is for 45- pushing 50-knot winds.

Quite suddenly, the thought of returning home and living the rest of my days not knowing if I could have climbed Everest if only I'd given it one more go was more than I could bear. I walked to John's tent, stooped and went inside. 'John,' I said, 'we must go.' And in a flash, as if a shadow of doubt had never crossed his mind, he was up like a Jack-in-a-box, out of his sleeping bag and ready.

It was four o'clock. Sacks packed, harnesses tied and crampons on our feet, we waved Sandy and Nawang goodbye and stepped onto the snowy glacier. Ang Passang and Kami Tchering would stay at Camp 2 and join us tomorrow on the Col. John led. He opted not to use oxygen, of which we had plenty, while I – thinking if you've got it, why not use it? – carried a large green British bottle. The Russian stuff we would keep for the Col.

We plodded along the path we had negotiated twice before across the head of the Western Cwm and towards the Lhotse Face. We hadn't gone far, only a few tens of yards, before John, ahead, was further ahead still. The distance grew, fifty yards, and then a hundred. 'John!' I cried, in panic. 'I'm dumping the oxygen.' Useless stuff, it weighed a ton. I unharnessed myself, laid the bottle beside the path in the snow and walked on, light-footed. Within minutes I had caught up with John; minutes again, and I was ahead, with John behind.

I walked easily that afternoon. 'I'll pace a hundred steps,' I muttered under my breath, and then rest. But I managed a hundred, two hundred, three, four, five hundred steps with no reason to stop. 'Are you all right?' I called back to John. 'No,' came the disgruntled cry. I waited. 'John, are you all right?' when he stood beside me. He said his legs were like jelly and let's go on. We went another hundred steps. He was still very tired. At a point just short of a crevasse – narrow enough that no ladder had been slung conveniently across it, yet too wide for a step, and requiring a skip and a jump to the other side – we sat down in the snow and, on a heavenly evening, the sun low in the sky, we considered our progress. John didn't think that he could go on, not at a satisfactory pace anyhow. Perhaps, he suggested, if he turned back, one of the Sherpas might walk up and accompany me? Or else, would I consider climbing on alone?

'Heavens! No, I wouldn't!' The idea filled me with horror! It was late. I would certainly be clambering up the ropes when it was dark. And as to whether or not there would be any neighbours on that precariously narrow perch up there on the lofty Lhotse Face, we thought not.

That left us with only the Sherpa option. Perhaps Ang Passang or Kami Tchering could set off on a rescue mission from Camp 2. We sat, the air still, the sun dipping lower in the sky, toying with this idea for a while. John was desperate that he should make the right decision. 'We'll have another go; just try another half an hour,' he said. But I think he knew there was little point.

It suddenly struck me how difficult this must be for him. John had rarely, if ever, had to turn his back on a physical challenge before: his heroism of a couple of days ago had debilitated him to the point at which his own chance of the summit had been lost.

He rootled in his sack for the radio and twiddled a few knobs to call Sandy at Camp 2. We would go with the Sherpa plan.

'I *think* you're suggesting . . .' said Sandy. We could hear him as clear as a bell. 'I *think* you're suggesting a Sherpa should leave tonight and join Becks. Over.' John repeated the message. 'Sorry, you're broken. Over.' Sandy got only the gist; we, his message, loud and all too clear: turn back, sleep at Camp 2 tonight, and me to climb to the South Col tomorrow. I didn't like that idea, but it seemed I had no choice. At least I would have gallons of Russian oxygen. I could plug in at Camp 2 if I liked. We got up and started back to camp, collecting our redundant British bottle on the way. It was only a few hundred yards.

At home in the warm, glowing red surroundings of our cook tent, Nawang tinkering with his pots and pans, Sandy looking on, John said to me, 'It'll be a monumental test of will.'

I was scared. I would be alone. I had never climbed on my own before. I'd hardly ever climbed without John. Tomorrow, as he reminded me, I would be taking on the biggest mountain in the world.

'But you won't be on your own,' said Sandy, all of a sudden persuasive. 'You'll be with Ang Passang and Kami Tchering, and Tcheri Zhambu.' The Sherpas were, without doubt, twice as strong and fast as any other man I had met on the hill, and always cheerful. But I was still worried in that I had never really climbed with them before.

'They know this mountain better than anyone,' said Sandy. Ang Passang and Kami Tchering had both been to the South Summit twice, maybe three times. 'And they're cautious,' he said. I felt ashamed. Sandy was right, of course. The Sherpas would look after me.

I was feeling a little more relaxed when, at supper, Peter's voice crackled into our cosy little gathering. 'Is this a good idea?' he asked. (Did I detect a touch of panic in his voice?) 'What does Rebecca intend doing when she reaches the South Col? People die up there, you know!'

I smiled, while John was cross. This was a mountaineering decision – *his* decision. What did Peter know about it?

Peter's fears abated, and he handed me over to have a brief word with David Fuller, who worked for the public relations company employed by our friends at DHL. I had not met him, only talked to him a couple of times on the satellite phone. I gathered he had been in contact with my mother. 'Understate it, won't you, to Mum?' I said. 'Please tell her I couldn't be in better hands.'

'I hear your message,' he said. And a decision had been made.

Chapter Eleven

————•·•··•——

I HEARD JOHN coughing through the night and I felt as though I had not slept a wink – though I must have – when at last there was a rustling about camp and it was time to move. It was 3.30 a.m. Nawang was up and about, already flashing up his stove, when John, Sandy, Ang Passang, Kami Tchering and Tcheri Zhambu hauled themselves out of their nice warm sleeping bags into the freezing cold darkness – just for me. I was touched.

The night's rest, though, had failed to shake off my despondency. I felt – despite everybody's efforts, the rethinking, repositioning of oxygen bottles, the radio calls – that the notion that we might succeed, and stand on Everest's snow-crested summit, was an impossibility. We all knew, I felt sure, that once on the South Col the winds would pick up and whistle us all the way down again. So, I asked, what is the point? Climbing at this altitude, above the clouds in such thin air, heavy boots and pack, lungs burning, gasping to catch breath to take even a single step is bearable just if you are quite certain that you are making headway. But if you feel you are walking into failure . . .

I sat, silent, a plate of rice on my lap. I love porridge but there was something about it at this altitude that I never did learn to stomach, so I had asked for rice – lots of carbohydrate smothered in large dollops of very yellow butter from a tin. It took me an age to eat it, forking up smaller and still smaller mouthfuls, delaying the inevitable. Tcheri Zhambu was ready and waiting, John and Sandy were waiting, and I knew that I had no choice if I wished to keep a modicum of pride. I could delay no longer.

It was five o'clock when the four of us – Ang Passang, Kami Tchering, Tcheri Zhambu and I – set off together from Camp 2, just as darkness was fading into day. As I turned to wave goodbye, I remembered what John had said of the climb: 'It'll be a monumental test of will.' And he was right – almost.

It wasn't the climb itself that was hard. Almost from the moment I stepped off the moraine on which our camp was pitched, and onto the snow-carpeted glacier in the Western Cwm, I found a rhythm, a lightness of foot and heart. I forgot my fear and climbed just for the hell of it. What *was* difficult was summoning the energy to pack my rucksack, struggle into my harness, boots, crampons, and set off up that hill once more.

Once on our way we travelled quickly, across the gently undulating glacier. I had an advantage in that I had one of those delectable little Russian oxygen bottles: compact, simple to use and, most important, light. I plugged in at Camp 2 and shot up the fixed ropes to Camp 3 in under four hours.

We stopped for a quick brew in our tent at Camp 3, perched on the tiniest snowy shelf between seracs, and then went on, up and across the Lhotse Face, to the Yellow Band. There was nothing special about this journey to the South Col that made it different from the last, except that the weather was only fair, not sunny, and we were alone, and not with a gathering from the United Nations. I felt a self-righteous smugness that I could keep up with the Sherpas, which was a nonsense, of course, because they carried no oxygen. Sadly, and off-puttingly, we had to walk past dear Lopsang's body. For days since the tragedy, we had watched a party of six or seven Sherpas patiently lower his body down the Lhotse Face from the Geneva Spur so that it could be cremated, as is the wish of Buddhists across his country. Tashi came into our tent one night. The Sherpas on the Lhotse Face were growing tired, he said, and needed a rest. He asked if we could spare our Sherpas to help lower his uncle from the Col. They were willing, of course, but, in the event, were not required, for the Sherpas who had accompanied Lopsang on the expedition, who for days had been lowering him patiently down, were also employees at the mountaineering institute where Lopsang was chief instructor in Darjeeling. And, tired though they were, they wanted to lower their friend all the way themselves. They had taken a rest, and left Lopsang, tethered to a rock, on a flattish piece of ground just above the Yellow Band; which was where Tcheri Zhambu and I had to walk past him. It was the saddest moment to look down on his body bag, picturing in my mind's eye, his smiling face, fortunately covered, for he had been cut and bruised in the fall, and to see his shape beneath the canvas. Tcheri Zhambu trotted past at a good speed and rested only when fifty or so yards the other side, while I followed, not wishing to dwell on the death of such a delightful man who had been so kind.

A couple of hours later we were over the crest of the Geneva Spur and walking the last leg along the rocky path towards the Col. It was one o'clock when we arrived. A climb that had previously taken two days had taken only eight hours, and we were last. Ang Passang and Kami Tchering were already in their tent, brewing us a drink.

I enjoyed watching them – they were so dexterous. The efficiency of their movements amazed me. The tent I shared with Tcheri Zhambu was full of snow, littered with food wrappings and crescent-shaped. It had once been domed – the last time I was in it, in fact – but the poles had buckled in the wind and the canvas collapsed. It was chaos, cold, unpleasant chaos, and yet Tcheri Zhambu managed to sort the oxygen, dry his feet, man the radio and half leave the tent to collect snow for a brew, all without knocking over the noodle soup warming on the stove in the corner. I mentioned in passing when I first entered the tent that my hands were cold. Tcheri Zhambu immediately whipped off my gloves, replaced them with his own dry ones, and rubbed them with a vigour extraordinary at this altitude, until he was happy that they were warm and I was cheerful again. When I took off my boots, socks steaming like a boiling kettle, he handed me his spare home-spun woolly ones and insisted that I put them on. I had to do nothing. He wouldn't allow me to, except to choose what I would like for supper. When I said I didn't mind, as long as it wasn't that awful boil-in-a-bag stuff, he produced from his rucksack a little plastic bag full of chapattis, which he toasted over a naked flame and which we ate with a little tuna fish.

That afternoon, spent in a grubby, snow-filled tent on a windswept plateau 3,000 feet below the summit of Everest, passed so contentedly. I was really happy, as long as I was cocooned in it with Tcheri Zhambu. As the afternoon wore on, I occasionally stuck my nose out through the zippered door, to see a line of scattered figures descend – triumphant, I assumed – from the summit. They were the Americans and the Indians, who had left Camp 2 the day before us. The thought of what lay ahead up that hill filled me with a crushing gloom.

One of the figures – just a black blob against the white – climbed slowly down the snow-filled gully and over the last band of ice and walked directly to our tent. It was Keith. When at last he had ripped off his oxygen mask and fought his rucksack off his back, he dropped to his knees, face drawn and grey, but eyes, wonderfully, still a sparkling blue, looked at me and said: 'Don't worry, baby, we still love you.'

I suspect that he, too, thought our chances slim, but he delivered a few words of encouragement: 'The weather might hold tonight,' he said. 'And if it's windy here on the Col, still give it a go; you climb out of the wind from here.'

'I hate the South Col,' I declared.

'Yes,' he said, 'but it looks one hell of a lot friendlier coming down,' and left, for a well-deserved sleep.

I had one thing to do before Tcheri Zhambu and I had a rest and that was to call John, at Camp 2, on the radio. 'Peter has the weather forecast in detail for you,' he said. 'It's a different forecast, and I'm afraid, gorgeous, a worse one than you originally had.'

'Becks?' It was Peter. 'The weather isn't as good as we want to have for you. We've spoken to Bracknell at length and they've given us some intermediate windspeeds for, literally, now, five o'clock local time. They say that it's gusting to 33 knots. The forecast then, for eleven o'clock, local time, tonight, is the wind picking up 35 to 40 knots and then tomorrow, going up to 45 knots.' He went on, all depressing news. 'It's not great,' he said. 'It's really not great. And tomorrow they're talking about thundery showers, so if you go up you've really got to get down fast before the really nasty weather comes in. Over.'

'Thanks, Peter. Over.'

All we could do was continue as planned. Seven p.m., and we put our heads down for two or three hours. The windward side of the tent had collapsed almost completely, so that we were sandwiched with the ground beneath and the canvas flapping around our knees. I couldn't sleep, just rested.

'Tcheri Zhambu,' I whispered, after a little time had passed.

He stirred.

'Tcheri Zhambu, there's no wind.' I could hardly believe it: the forecast was as wrong as it was possible to be.

Tcheri Zhambu sat bolt upright. It was 10 p.m., we planned to leave at 11 p.m. He lit the stove for a brew. It takes a while, as I had discovered, to collect and melt snow, but an hour or so passed and I got the distinct impression that something was up. The Sherpas, Ang Passang and Kami Tchering in the other tent, and Tcheri Zhambu with me, were talking among themselves in Nepali.

'What's going on?' I asked Tcheri Zhambu.

'Weather's not good.'

'But there's no wind,' I retorted. I stuck my head out of the tent: the mountain was as clear as a bell, the sky crowded with stars.

'Ang Passang says black cloud in valley. Too dangerous.'

'Well,' I mused, 'the perfect excuse.' A large part of me thought: I can go back to bed, put my head down, forget the whole bloody thing. I could live with failure, I thought, if it was the weather not I that dictated it. But another part of me still wanted that summit. There was only one thing left to do. I put on my boots, tripped out of our tent and into theirs.

'Ang Passang?'

'Black cloud,' he said. 'We're young.'

'Ang Passang, pass the radio, please.' John and Sandy had said to me that they would be sleeping in the cook tent that night, by the radio, so I could call them at any time. I was touched. The boys at Base Camp were doing the same.

I explained. 'John, Ang Passang just keeps saying it's dangerous. He says the cloud is too black, we may not find our way, and there's lightning. You have a view on that?'

'I don't know, Becks.' This was desperate. 'The weather's going to get worse, not necessarily in the next two hours, but it's going to build up. Whether it will hold off long enough I wouldn't like to say,' said John.

The discussion went round in circles: Camp 4 to Camp 2, Camp 2 to Base Camp, and back to Camp 4. Everyone threw in their bit. Everyone was up, it seemed: John, Noel, our *sirdar* Ang Phurba, the Sherpas at Base Camp. It was snowing lower down the hill – might be the edge of the storms on the North Indian plane, it's monsoonish, they said. Yes, black clouds are thunderclouds, and thunderstorms often strike ridges. But it was clear up there now, black only in the valley. 'Talk it over very gently with Ang Passang and let him make the final decision,' said John. 'It's his life too.'

The message that I was receiving from my team mates was thunderingly loud and clear: 'We want you to succeed, Rebecca. We want, desperately, for you to get to the top, but we don't want to be responsible if you die.' And who could blame them? John displayed remarkable courage that night. He is a leader. He has led all his life, in the Royal Marines, at Plas y Brenin, on mountains. This time he was leading on the largest mountain of all, but not from the front, as he would have liked, and as he was used to, but from 4,000 feet down the hill. I knew, of course, that I wouldn't die: I felt this with the assurance a seasoned traveller feels when boarding a plane. But the reality of the situation was disquieting. Three people had died in the two months we had been on Everest, each one where we were about to go – at above 26,000 feet, in the Death Zone. How on earth would John feel if he encouraged us to go and we did not return?

We waited an hour. The wind did not pick up and the stars still crowded the sky. Then I saw three little head-torches making their way up the hill from the Col. I remembered now: I had seen three figures far behind, as we climbed the Lhotse Face. Must be them. I don't know how the decision was made, but one thing was sure: if those three people thought there might be even the slimmest chance of making the summit, I could not go back to bed.

It was 12.30 a.m. and we were ready to go: water-bottles full, chocolate, gloves, glasses, radio, crampons on, ice-axe in hand, oxygen on back, mask on face. 'Get on those ropes,' said John. 'Get onto the South Summit. Reassess the situation there. And good luck. I think you're going to be OK. Over.'

I heard him switch to Base Camp. 'The beauty of fixed ropes,' he said, 'is that you can't get lost. If the worst comes to the worst they can just turn round and rattle down the ropes back to the tent.'

Kami Tchering, Ang Passang, Tcheri Zhambu and I walked into the darkness, one behind the other. I was the lucky one. Each of the Sherpas carried a large British oxygen bottle and I had a little Russian one. They switched on to only 1 litre per minute, for fear, I think, of running dry, while I, with plenty, afforded 3 litres per minute. The extra oxygen and the lighter weight more than compensated for my feebleness compared with the Sherpas, and I kept pace, even felt relaxed, as we puffed a rhythmic breath the hundred yards or so across the rocky, snow-encrusted plateau towards the icy band that lay between it and the gully that rose, awesome, above.

From afar, the icy band, convex, bulbous, looked like glass. It had an inauspicious blue sheen that spelt hard, brittle ice, and indeed it was, but it was impregnated in places with little pebbles that made the going easier. A keen eye could pick out boot-sized steps in the otherwise steepish ground, pricked with the traces of numerous pairs of crampons that had passed this way before us. These we followed, Kami Tchering and Ang Passang at a steady pace, Tcheri Zhambu, behind, more slowly. I hung back. He was coughing, on and on, as if a fishbone was stuck in his throat. 'Tcheri Zhambu?' Still he coughed. 'I go back,' he said. It was agonizing just listening to him. 'But not here!' I cried. We were slap in the middle of a particularly nasty slippery bit. 'Climb to the top of the ice, where it's safe, and we can talk.'

But when we were safe, there was little need for discussion. He was going, he said, there was no way that he could carry on. He dropped his rucksack so that we could transfer the spare Russian bottle from his sack into mine. 'Thank you, Tcheri Zhambu, thank you for everything,' I said, and waved him goodbye, a lonely figure in the darkness.

I wonder if John would have been happy to let us go on if

he had known what we were to discover as the ground steepened and we entered the foot of the gully that led straight up the face, and to the right, onto the South East Ridge. There were no fixed ropes – or if there were, we didn't find them. They must have been buried under the snow. It was very dark. And to add to the fun I had let my head-torch batteries run flat, as had Ang Passang. Kami Tchering led, turning his head every few paces so we could follow.

It was much steeper than I had imagined and icy in patches. In other places rock lay camouflaged under the thinnest powdering of snow. Crampons scraped, and slipped. I wondered at times how the hell we were going to get down again. But for the moment we were heading up. Kami Tchering took a few steps; Ang Passang followed him, and I went behind him. We rested, leaning on our ice-axes, like old men bent over walking-sticks. Once when we were in this position we looked eastward, and saw in the night sky a brilliant yellow light, flickering mysteriously like a candle-flame. I watched, intrigued, as it grew larger and larger; and then realized, rather stupidly, that what we were gazing at was the moon: a plump, sickle moon. And in the valleys far below us in Tibet, lightning flashed.

On we went. The three lights ahead were a little closer now, and I could see, above, in the shadows, a snowy passage between rocks leading diagonally to the right, towards the ridge. We're doing rather well, I thought. We're making progress. But the Sherpas, I learnt, felt otherwise. It was about 4 a.m., still dark, and they sat down in the snow on a precarious shelf by a large rock and refused to budge.

'What's the matter, guys?'

They were chatting away on the radio in Nepali. I took

the radio. 'Becks?' It was John. 'Nawang says you've got two cold scared Sherpas.' Well, perhaps. Thin cloud now engulfed us and the stars were no longer visible. 'Maybe if you can persuade them to keep going until dawn, that might do the trick,' he said.

Maybe. 'Look, Ang Passang, let's just keep climbing until we catch up with the three ahead. We can discuss it with them.' I tried everything. 'Take my jacket.' (I carried a spare one in my sack.) 'If you get to the top? Yes, of course you can come to London.'

They were reluctant, but eventually they – we – moved on. We never did discuss it with the three climbers ahead. We caught up with them, for they, without oxygen, were climbing slowly, said hello and climbed on past.

It was hard work, harder for the Sherpas than for me on only one litre of oxygen per minute. The gradient was a little kinder on the traverse to the ridge, but the snow was a little deeper. I couldn't take more than six or seven steps in succession. I tried – ten steps, I promised, next time – but I never did, except for once, without oxygen. The tubing that ran from the oxygen bottle to the mask had a little valve, encased in a transparent shell so that you could see at a glance if the gas was flowing or not. It was a device designed to show when a change of bottle was required, and was totally superfluous. My oxygen didn't run out on a flat bit of ground, cushioned with a soft blanket of snow, or even where it was gently sloping, where I could have taken off my rucksack and changed the bottle relatively easily. It happened on the steepest bit of mixed rock and snow we had yet encountered on that traverse from snow-gully to ridge. I was fighting for breath instantly as if my face had been smothered with a pillow. Looking up, a few yards above, I saw my salvation: a platform of snow. In a panic, ice-axe swinging, crampons flying, I scurried up to it with the speed of the devil. I landed in a heap, gasping for every breath as if it was my last, thinking my ribcage would implode.

Bottle changed and sunglasses on, for flat morning light now pervaded the valley, and we climbed on, up steep but easier ground, onto the ridge. We stopped to rest for a while, and gazed down on the South Col, far, far below. Looking up, we were able to see the South East Ridge for the first time from the eastern side, sweeping high and gently to our right. It was at once breathtaking, and daunting, for it looked a hell of a way to climb.

The snow was deep and fresh on the ridge, and lacking any hint of footsteps left by climbers who had passed this way before us. It was a high, beautiful wilderness, and we were alone.

We took it in turns to kick steps in the snow, Kami Tchering leading, and when he was tired, Ang Passang, and when he was tired, it was down to me. A light snow blew in our faces. The whole of Tibet was one ominous snowcloud, nothing but an ethereal wall of pale grey; and I worried a little that the cloud might blow over and visibility deteriorate. The nagging doubt that afflicts all mountaineers from time to time – should we climb on or should we turn back? – haunted me every step of the way, but we climbed on, until somewhere along the South East Ridge leading to the South Summit the Sherpas' attitude changed. No words were spoken, but I knew, as if by osmosis, that they, too, wanted to climb to the summit.

It took an age to climb that ridge, hour after hour, and I

didn't know when it would come to an end. Whereas six, maybe seven steps in succession had been possible lower down, here the snow was deeper, the altitude higher, the air thinner, and it was impossible to take more than one, sometimes two steps, without bending over double from the waist, to recover breath, and rest. Each step was a monumental effort of will, requiring a kick, and another kick, to secure a footing and ensure you didn't slide with the soft snow down again to where you had started.

'Up there, South Summit,' the Sherpas pointed. On we went. Where it was particularly steep, the underlying rock lay exposed and, half on this rock, half on snow, we trod carefully, slowly picking a route up the ridge, until finally the gradient eased and the rock once again lay hidden deep under the snow, and the going became a little less precarious.

At this point I was leading, and made my way round and up a snowy knoll to the top of what I knew to be the highest point we had viewed from the South Col, far below: the South Summit, 28,750 feet up in the sky. It was a marvellous moment. The snowy summit was comfortably large, and flat. I felt no fear, no worry of some careless, fatal slip. I could sit in the snow, as I did, and gaze upon the world stretched beneath me. And I was alone, quite alone. For a few moments the view, down into my beloved Western Cwm, to Nuptse's crenellated ridge, to the monster that was Lhotse, and beyond, to Pumori, to Cho Oyu, far in the west, was all mine.

I rootled in my rucksack, and called John. 'It's warm!' I cried. Well, it wasn't warm exactly, but not cold either, with oxygen, swaddled in layer upon layer of fleece and down. 'There are sort of little whirlwinds of snow, but the wind isn't strong. I can put my gloves down without worrying about them.' In a fit of extravagance I had just switched up my oxygen to 4 litres per minute; I thought I could afford it, just for the final push. 'So,' I said, 'I'm feeling fine, I'm feeling great! But I feel sorry for the Sherpas; they're on two litres per minute now. Over.'

'Becks, we heard that perfectly. That's great news. I suppose the Sherpas can't turn theirs up any, can they? Over.'

'They've only got one British cylinder each. Over.' And this was a dilemma, for their British masks were incompatible with my Russian bottles.

We chatted a while, John and I, about ridges, snowy bumps and Hillary's Step. It was the most elevated conversation I'm ever likely to have! 'How far behind you are the Sherpas?' he asked.

'Well, I can't see them now, but there's a ridge not very far away. Over.'

He went on, 'Peter's got a telephone conversation lined up with your mum when you're on the top, if you've got the energy and the time.'

This threw me. 'If – ah, here come the Sherpas – if I have a conversation with Mum, do I need the New Zealand radio? Over.'

'Yes, course you do, you dope. Over.'

'Well, I hope the Sherpas have got it. It wouldn't work last night. Over.'

'OK, well your mum will never forgive you, but we will.' And that was that, over.

It was about 11.00 a.m. Together we planted my half-used oxygen bottle in the snow, to be collected on our return, and replaced it with a new, full one so that there would be no need to carry a spare, and walked to the summit ridge. I don't know why: I had read hundreds of books and talked to countless people, and yet when I first set eyes on the view along that final ridge towards the summit, it staggered me. Everything we had climbed thus far had been snow and ice, with just a little smidgen of rock peeping through here and there. What lay ahead was rock, mostly: large angular lumps, falling away abruptly, left and right. To the left it falls sharply away, 6,000 feet into Nepal; and to the right, even more sharply, if that's possible, the 9,000 feet of the Kangshung Face, into Tibet.

'You can go first, Kami Tchering,' I said.

'No, you can go.'

'No, you go.'

Kami Tchering led, down a little gully and onto the ridge. It wasn't difficult by Alpine standards; I'd heard it said it was a mere *peu difficile*, but it was about as exposed as you can get. This was Hillary Step territory. I could see it ahead: a large rhomboid boulder standing on its head, complicated with slabs and cornices all about. But first we had to inch our way along the ridge to that point. On closer inspection, it seemed that for most of the way we could follow a passage on snow. On the right, huge cornices, beaten and swept into shape by the prevailing westerly winds, jutted out like great snowy waves over the 9,000-foot drop into Tibet. And from the tips of these waves, the ridge, snow for the most, dropped steeply to join the edge of the rocks atop the western face, falling into Nepal. Along this, we climbed, grabbing a rock hold with our clumsy mittened hands where we could, checking and double checking each step to ensure its stability. Climb too high to the right, stick an ice-axe into the snow for balance, and it would enter in Nepal, to exit the other side of the cornice in Tibet. Climb too low to the left and, well, there was nothing. There were fixed ropes in parts, into which I diligently clipped my harness; but where there were not, one slip and it would all have been over.

Within an hour or so, perhaps less, we were at the foot of Hillary's Step. This, Harry had said, was so nondescript that you could climb it without noticing it. In a pair of plimsolls, perhaps; on a warm summer's afternoon, in shorts, bare-fingered, perhaps. But at nearly 29,000 feet, in heavy boots, hands rendered into useless clubs by vast gloves, ice-axe swinging, goggles steaming up, I beg to differ.

A bunch of old tat hung like a knotted loop of multicol-oured spaghetti, from some unseen anchor. I grabbed it, pulled, and with a series of inelegant kicks, tugs, pushes, rams and elbow shoves, jostled and heaved my clumsy self onto a sloping mantel, the top of the rhomboid, I suppose, some two-thirds of the way up the Step. From here it was relatively simple: I planted my axe into a snowy shelf above, and scrambled.

I was glad when we left the rockier part of the ridge behind, for ahead, as before, cornices swept in vast, frozen waves to the right, and steep rocky slopes fell away to the left, into Nepal; the ridge was broader than before, though, more gently inclined, a little kinder. It undulated on, as ridges tend to do, one bump, then another, and another.

But there was an air of confidence among us now and despite fatigue, thin air, the effort required to put one foot in front of the other, and the implausibility of us climbing together on the summit ridge of this, Everest, the most majestic mountain of them all, we knew now that we would make it to the summit. And we knew the moment we were about to arrive, for there, ahead, was the highest bump of them all with lots of flags on top. We stood and waited until the three of us were huddled in a little cluster, and together stepped on top of the world. It wasn't very dramatic but the joy on the Sherpas' faces made my heart near burst: 'Summit, summit, summit. We make summit!'

I suppose it is fear that forbids one to bask too long in such moments. The cloud cleared to reveal a view across the Tibetan plateau that stretched for miles: to China and Mongolia, no doubt. Looking down, I could see the great white Rongbuk glacier, winding along the valley floor from the foot of the mountain on the northern side. I had been looking forward to that: I knew every inch of the glacier from my first expedition on Everest in 1989. And there, far below, on the lateral moraine, in the shadow of Changtse, was where we had pitched our Advanced Base Camp, and across the way, Bill's Buttress on Everest's North East Ridge, where for the first time in my life I had put on crampons and a harness, and held an ice-axe, and set foot on a mountain. It felt a perfectly circular and complete story.

But I only glanced for a second. I took off my rucksack, my oxygen mask, my gloves, and together we posed for a photograph. It was cold. The wind had picked up a little and with only thin liner gloves, and no oxygen, I was losing body heat fast. We must go. I switched my oxygen to 3 litres per minute – four would have been nice, but it had taken us an hour and a half from South Summit to summit true, and on the higher flow rate the bottle lasted only three hours. I didn't want to risk running dry.

It was exhausting going down; I knew it would be. And I knew it was dangerous too. The three people who had died this season, died here, descending from the summit to the Col.

So I concentrated hard. The Sherpas were wonderful beyond words. 'Slowly, slowly,' they said. Kami Tchering led, while Ang Passang paced himself just behind me.

It took about five hours to get down, and for an hour of that time the snowcloud that had so ominously filled Tibet invaded our path and masked our vision almost completely. I could only see the red blob that was Kami Tchering just ahead. The ground was a nothingness, and we had to feel what might be beneath us with our ice-axes and feet, as if we were blind. I thought for the only time in the two months we had been on Everest that our luck might finally have run out. But I felt strangely calm. I wasn't scared. I knew that there was nothing we could do about it, except to feel our way forward and down.

The snow, freshly fallen, was deep. When the cloud finally cleared, looking down upon the South East Ridge we could see no hint of the footsteps we had left when we were scrambling up, and the ridge looked narrower, somehow, than it had before. One slip to the left and we would have whistled down the Kangshung Face to land, for ever, in a snowy burial ground in Tibet. So I resisted the temptation to slide down the ridge on my bottom, or to take long confident strides like a polar bear romping in the snow. I didn't dare. Each step I took slowly, deliberately, with painful care, until at last I collapsed exhausted just above where the ridge adjoins the path that we were to follow down the south face to the Col. Here I stopped: my legs were jelly and my stomach so empty I felt sure it would shatter and cave in like a paper-thin ceramic pot. 'We go, South Col before dark,' said Ang Passang. 'Not,' I said, 'until I have had a drink.' And slowly I drew out my water-bottle, deep inside my down suit to keep it warm, and swigged the last few precious drops.

Refreshed – just a little fuel in the empty tank and I felt revitalized – I followed Kami Tchering along the remains of the ridge, along the crest here, kicking steps along a knife-edge of snow, and right, along the diagonally sloping passage that led into the gully above the Col. The fresh snow was a help here, providing a soft cushion over the icy patches I had worried about descending, when we were climbing up. Still, I slipped twice, grinding to a halt with the aid of my ice-axe. The going was steep; we were exhausted, and the wind that blew more furiously with every step cut into our faces. But, far below, I could see a small scarlet figure, on the Col, excitedly waving his arms. It was Tcheri Zhambu.

Half an hour later and he was unstrapping the crampons from my feet and rubbing my hands warm. He had boiled some noodle soup, but I wasn't in the mood for eating; and so he offered to make me just a drink, but I wasn't in the mood for drinking either. Not even when a billy of hot coffee was presented to me by a boisterous, smiling Basque. He and his companion, who was lying sick in his tent, were the only round-eyes around, as far as I could make out. 'Here,' he said, handing me the radio. 'It's for you.'

'John! Yes, I'm fine.'

'Are you sure?'

'Yes, really, I'm fine.' And I was, just so long as I wasn't taking one more step either up or down that hill. 'Could you do me a favour?' I asked. 'Just one favour. I know it's silly, but is there any chance Peter could make a call home, tell them I'm OK?'

'I think,' he said, 'you'll find that done,' or some such reassuring words.

Ang Passang and Kami Tchering weren't hanging around. Like the wind, they were off, down the fixed rope to the sheltered corner of the Western Cwm. But I wasn't going anywhere that night. Another step, and I thought I would be inviting some misadventure; with Tcheri Zhambu, I crawled into our crescent-shaped tent on the South Col. Dear Tcheri Zhambu. His face oozed warmth, generosity and goodwill – and I knew that he had passionately wanted to join us that day. He insisted that I climbed into my sleeping bag and rested; but I couldn't sleep – not that it mattered. Nothing mattered that night. It occurred to me that not once in our five-hour descent had I afforded myself the luxury of thinking that I had just climbed to the top of the world. The concentration of putting one foot slowly in front of the other had been too great. Only now that the storm which had threatened to scupper our chances had finally struck, the wind whistling around the tent, the poles buckling still further and the canvas flapping, did I stop to think that at this final hour we had completed what we had set out to do. I lay, Tcheri Zhambu asleep at my side, and realized that for the first time in my thirty-one years I was quietly, deeply content. Everest had been my first mountain, and surely not my last.

Epilogue

———•••———

If our ascent of Everest was a slow and, in many ways, a troubled one, our descent, and my journey on to Kathmandu, and home, must have been the fastest in the history of Everest. Ang Passang, Kami Tchering and I stood on the summit on Monday 17 May. The following Saturday I was with the team at a press conference at the Royal Geographical Society in London. I resented this a little. I had assumed, wrongly, that I would be able to amble down slowly, and sleep; and had dreamt, that last night on the Col, of wandering as free as the air through the foothills, tucking into a feast of scrumptious cakes in Kathmandu, shopping a little, buying trinkets for family and friends, and relaxing, perhaps, still skinny, on some heavenly beach in Thailand. But the sponsors dictated otherwise, and seeing as they had paid our ticket – well, it would have been churlish not to have complied with their wishes.

A mountain that had taken us a couple of months to climb, took us a day to descend. I was exhausted, physically weak – and overjoyed. One of my warmest memories is of staggering into our camp at the head of the Western Cwm and falling into the arms of John and Sandy, waiting patiently all this time, and then into the arms of Nawang, the cook, who hugged me so hard, so tight, that I thought my feet would never again touch the ground. Together in a little line we walked the length of the Western Cwm and for the third and final time down the 'tumbled labyrinth' where, half-way through, we saw a couple of the young cook-boys coming towards us, laden with flasks of hot sweet lemon and tea. A little further, along the wiggly path to Base Camp and there, in a cluster, stood Peter, Dave, Noel, Sandy, Brian, Wyn, Ang Phurba and his team of Sherpas, beers in hand, welcoming us home. Their generosity of spirit was overwhelming.

We stayed only a day at Base Camp. To meet our deadline, we had to walk the five or so hours to Pheriche, where, at 14,000 feet, a helicopter would whisk us away to Kathmandu, to meet our flight to London. My legs moved as if with a will of their own, striding, through barriers of pain and fatigue, down the hill towards our destination; they moved with an energy borrowed from days, weeks that were to come – but my spirit soared. The high mountains are a lifeless place: beautiful, but sterile. They are a place to visit, to wonder at, to admire and respect, and to seek adventure – but not a place to live. My eyes had grown weary of the stark shades of blue and grey and white; they had been starved of the colours of life, and now, as we strode down the valley, losing height with every step, we walked from winter into summer in a day. We stepped, with joy, off the glacier on to soft, bouncy turf; brooks bubbled; there were moss, lichen and grass, and between individual blades, the tiniest Himalayan flowers. Yak calves frolicked in the fields.

We slept a night in a smoky teahouse in Pheriche and in the morning, chatting over omelettes and mugs of chocolate

or tea, we heard, at first far away and then booming overhead, the throbbing whir of propellers. The helicopter didn't
stop, just hovered long enough for us to scurry on board and
be lifted into the sky. In that moment, 'Life doesn't get much
more exciting than this!' I cried.

One more sensuous pleasure before home: a long-awaited
complete body overhaul. We stopped for four hours in a
Kathmandu hotel before departure, just long enough for a
self-indulgent visit to the beauty parlour. 'The lot, please,' I
said, and sat myself down for a hair-wash and cut, facial,
manicure, pedicure – and a glorious full body massage. Ah,
to feel human! It didn't last. A long night's journey and we
were taxiing on the runway at Heathrow. I can't explain how
strange, how distant, how unreal it feels to hear your name
tannoyed on a plane, to be ushered into a secret room, to be
divested of passport and luggage, and to be told, quite matter-
of-factly, 'The paparazzi await.'

Our duties over, we drifted into the lush garden of the
Royal Geographical Society. My mother was there, my sister,
her husband and her kids, and loads of friends. Children
skipped under the laburnum tree. Life is rich for contrasts.
The last time I had laid down my head to sleep was on a
wooden bench a fortnight's walk from a road, high in the
Himalayas. The following day, with an old friend, I bathed in
the sunshine in a London park, took a stroll along the Fulham
Road, saw a film and stopped for a pizza and a bottle of
wine.

Such delights, such acute appreciation of the small
pleasures that make up our everyday lives, sadly fade. But
other joys of my Himalayan adventure I will never lose. I will
never forget climbing for the first time into the heaven's gate

that is the Western Cwm, or sitting, alone, on the South Summit, looking down on the world stretched beneath me. I will never forget stepping on top of the world with Ang Passang and Kami Tchering. Without them – the childlike joy on their faces – it would have been a lonely affair. I shall never forget Tcheri Zhambu and how he looked after me to the end. And I shall never forget the support of every other Sherpa and member of the British 40th Anniversary Everest Expedition. There is not one who was not instrumental to my success. I was lucky to be invited to be a part of such a team, that the organization was impeccable, that on the day of reckoning, the storm held off just long enough to allow us to climb up and, more important, safely down again. I was lucky to have opportunity to fulfil my dream.

Glossary

Abseil   A quick way to descend a steep rock face or ice wall using a doubled rope, which is secured around a rock, ice bollard or peg. The climber makes a controlled slide down the face, and pulls the rope down after him or her.

Acclimatization   At high altitudes the air is 'thin' (lacking oxygen) and the human body must adapt to the different air quality and pressure. Breathing becomes deeper and faster, the heart rate is raised and the blood thickens due to the multiplication of red blood cells and lower plasma levels. The speed of acclimatization varies but the safest course is to gain height gradually and not stay at high altitudes for long. Most Everest climbers suffer acclimatization symptoms, which include headaches, insomnia, nausea and, more rarely, pulmonary or cerebral oedema.

Avalanche   The movement of snow and other surface material (ice, earth, rocks) from a mountain side.

Belaying   The safeguarding of climbers by securing them to an anchor.

Col   A dip in a ridge, often between two peaks.

Cornice   An overhanging mass of hardened snow at the edge of a precipice.

Couloir   A steep gully (q.v.).

Crampons   Steel spikes which fit over the soles of a boot used for climbing ice or snow.

Crevasse   Often concealed by snow, a crack in the surface of a glacier.

Duvet   Eiderdown used to make jackets, trousers and all-in-one suits.

Fixed ropes   Ropes which remain fixed on difficult parts of the route throughout an expedition as an aid to climbing and transporting equipment.

Frostbite   At very low temperatures ice crystals form between cells, usually those in the extremities of the body (nose, feet, hands, lips, ears) and blood vessels constrict. Oxygen supply is impeded, leading to infection and deterioration. In serious cases, an affected area may have to be amputated.

Glacier   A river of ice fed by seasonal snow, which flows down a valley.

Gully   A fissure in a mountainside.

Ice-axe   An essential tool when climbing in snow and ice. Usually it has a spike at the end of its shaft and a double head: one in the shape of a pick, the other in the shape of an adze.

Icefall   An icefall forms when a glacier moves over a steep declivity. The ice fractures, creating fissures and pinnacles. It must be negotiated carefully as the downward movement of the glacier makes it unstable.

Jumar   A metal device clipped to a rope which moves upwards but cannot slip down.

Karabiner   An oval metal ring, with spring clip or screw gate. Also called 'krab'.

La   Tibetan word for col or pass.

Mixed climbing   Climbing partly on snow and partly on rock.

Moraine   The mass of earth and rock material pushed aside by a glacier as it moves down a valley.

Oedema   Acute altitude sickness where fluid accumulates on the lungs (pulmonary) or on the brain (cerebral). Retreat to lower altitudes is imperative for recovery. The condition can be fatal.

Overhang   Layer of rock or ice jutting over the vertical face.

Pass   A passage between one valley and another.

Pitch   The distance between two anchors.

Piton   A metal pin hammered into a crack in the rock (or ice), used as an anchor or runner.

Ridge   The line of junction of two opposing faces of a mountain.

Rib   A small ridge on the face of a mountain.

Rope   Originally made of silk or hemp, ropes are now made of nylon or perlon. These materials are more resistant and fare better in low temperatures.

Scree   A slope of loose stones.

Serac   An ice pinnacle.

Sherpa   Tibetan in origin, these people settled in the Solu Khumbu area near Everest as well as in Darjeeling and Kathmandu.

Sirdar   Head Sherpa on an expedition.

Slab   A sheet of rock on a steep gradient.

Sling   A loop of rope or nylon tape.

Snow-blindness   Temporary and painful blindness caused by reflected light from a glacier or snowfield.

Snow bridge   A bridge of snow crossing a crevasse, the reliability of which is often difficult to judge.

Snow cave   A cave dug in the snow for temporary shelter.

Steps   Footholds cut into the ice with an ice axe or into snow with the boot.

Traverse   To climb roughly horizontally across a feature.

Wall   An extremely steep face of rock or ice.

THE DHL BRITISH 40TH ANNIVERSARY EVEREST EXPEDITION 1993 – MEMBERS

John Barry
Bill Barker
Noel Bristow
Peter Earl
Dr Chris Fenn
Brian Freeland
Dave Halton
Wyn Jones

Dr Andy Peacock
Jan (John) Rowe
Lincoln Rowe
Dr Sandy Scott
Sandy Simpson
Rebecca Stephens
Harry Taylor
Dave Walsh

THE DHL BRITISH 40TH ANNIVERSARY EVEREST EXPEDITION 1993 – SPONSORS

The following companies generously supported the expedition by supplying equipment, clothing, services or food:

AMS Ltd
Apple Computer UK Ltd
Bodystat Ltd of the Isle of Man
Bolle
Boots Foods
Bridgedale
Buffalo
Florida Caribbean Manufacturing
Canon
Central Studios Ltd
Crooks Health Care Ltd
CPC (UK) Best Foods Ltd
DHL International (UK) Limited
DMM

Justin de Blank Foods Limited
Dunlop
EPI Gas
Everfresh Natural Foods
Fuji
Fulwell Mill Company (The)
Grampian Oat Products
Halina
Hamlyns
Health and Diet Company
Health and Nutrition Centre
H. J. Heinz Co. Ltd
Helly Hansen (UK) Ltd
Hollymill Bakery

Icom (UK) Ltd
IDB Mobile Communications
Ilford Ltd
Jack Daniels
Jacobs and Co (Liverpool) Ltd
Jordan W (Cereals) Ltd
H. Young Holdings
Karrimor International Ltd
Knorr
Kodak
Konica
Lifestream Research U.K.
Llewelyn Wynne
Lyon Equipment
MacDonald & Muir (Glenmorangie)
Marconi Marine
McVities Ltd
Mitchelhill Biscuit Factory
Mountain Equipment
Needlers PLC
Nestlé Rowntree
Nikon
Patagonia UK Ltd
Perseverance Mills Ltd

Phileas Fogg
Philips
Polaroid
Rab Down Equipment
RoC
Reebok
Shepherd Boy Ltd
Smith
SECA Ltd
Simmers
Smith & Nephew
Sony
John Smith & Sons (New Pitsligo) Ltd
Sunnyvale
Super Chrome Services Ltd
Taymar Ltd
Thai International Airways
Troll
Walkers Shortbread Ltd
Weetabix Ltd
Whitworths Ltd
Wholebake
Wild Country

And the following, cash:

Abtrain
Alsop Wilkinson
Astra Pharmaceuticals
BDO Siedman
Bridon Charitable Trust
Business Research Unit, Robert
   Gordon University
Carter Organization, Inc. (The)
D.H. & A.D. Fitzwilliam-Lay
DHL International (UK) Limited
Foundation for Sports and the Arts

Justin de Blank Foods Limited
MacDonald & Muir (Glenmorangie)
Neville Shulman
Quorum Communications UK
Randall Corwin
Sally Ferries
Siegel Sommers & Schwartz
Siedman & Siedman Foundation
Sloane Corporate Finance Limited
Uni-Vite Nutrition Ltd

Our thanks to all these companies and individuals for their generosity.